W9-BTE-755

STUDIES IN AFRICAN HISTORY · 3

Swahili
The Rise of a National Language

TO THE MEMORIES OF
H. E. LAMBERT AND SHAABEN ROBERT
FOR WHOM SWAHILI REMAINED ALWAYS A HERITAGE,
A REALITY AND AN IDEAL

WILFRED WHITELEY

SWAHILI

The Rise of a National Language

METHUEN & CO LTD
11 New Fetter Lane · London EC4

WINGATE COLLEGE LIBRARY
WINGATE. N. C.

First published 1969 by Methuen & Co Ltd
© Wilfred Whiteley 1969
Printed in Great Britain by
Richard Clay (The Chaucer Press) Ltd
Bungay, Suffolk

SBN (casebound) 416 10850 4
SBN (paperback) 416 10870 9

This title is available in both hard and paperback editions. The paperback edition is sold subject to the condition that it shall not, by way of trade or otherwise, be lent, re-sold, hired out, or otherwise circulated without the publisher's prior consent in any form of binding or cover other than that in which it is published and without a similar condition including this condition being imposed on the subsequent purchaser.

Distributed in the United States by
Barnes & Noble Inc

Contents

Preface   *page* vii

I   Language and Literature   1

II   Early History   28

III   The Diffusion Up-country   42

IV   The Colonial Period   57

V   'Standard' Swahili   79

VI   After Independence   97

VII   Problems of a National Language   114

Notes   129

Select Bibliography on Swahili Language   141

Index   146

44689

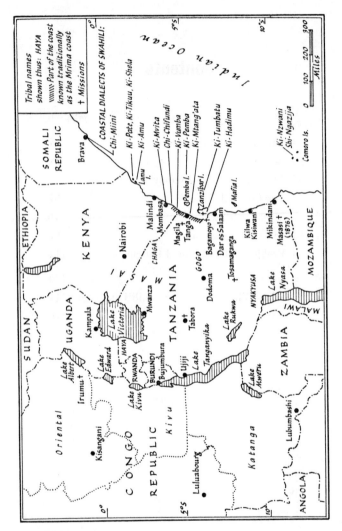

MAP OF EASTERN AFRICA
showing the main places and dialects noted in the text

Preface

My aim in this book has been to make a modest contribution to the study of language choice. What are the factors which at different historical periods have led people to use one language rather than another, or, within a given period, to use a particular language in one set of circumstances and another one in a different set? As yet we know little about such factors, though our knowledge is growing fast, and should be increased substantially by the activities of such projects as the recently set up Survey of Language Use and Language Teaching in Eastern Africa.

Swahili probably owes something initially to the unknown historical factors which led groups of people speaking broadly similar languages to be dispersed over a wide geographical area within sight of the sea. Such linguistic affinity between people engaged in coastal trading would serve both to promote the trade and the development of a common form of the language. When a locality served by such a common means of communication develops as a focal point for that trade, as did Zanzibar during the first part of the nineteenth century, then the language is ideally placed to take advantage of this. But Swahili owes something, too, to the energy and initiative of caravan leaders like Tippu Tip, and also to the reputation of groups like the Masai, who for many years prevented the penetration of Kenya and Uganda by any but the most circuitous routes. If the caravans, trading settlements, and missions had not paved the way for the widespread use of Swahili would the German administration have made the same choice or would there have been the same kind of indecision as has characterized language choice in Kenya? Swahili is also indebted to the single-mindedness of those who carried through the programme of standardization in the thirties and forties, to enable the politicians of the fifties to use it as the language of national unity. Now, in the sixties, it seems that the language is poised to emerge as the most dynamic modern language of Africa. Whether it does so depends on the attitudes of East Africans, whether they will choose it as the most suitable means of communication for the complex reality of life in this part of the twentieth century. The book therefore begins, as it will end, with a question.

In the writing of it I have been constantly made aware of my debts to others: Chapter II owes much to the work of my friend Dr G. S. P. Freeman-Grenville. If I disagree with him over the interpretation of the historical evidence for Swahili, the fact that I can do so at all is due to his pioneering studies, and I am grateful to him for reading the early chapters and for discussing with me the problems they raise. Chapter III owes much to the work of Sir John Gray, again a distinguished pioneer. Chapter IV contains material from my earlier articles 'The Changing Position of Swahili in East Africa', *Africa*, Vol. XXVI, 1956, 343–53, and 'Language and Politics in East Africa', *Tanganyika Notes*, 47/48, 1957, 159–73. To the editors of these journals I am grateful for permission to reproduce this material. Part of Chapter VI is taken from a paper I delivered at Airlie House, Va., in November 1966 to a Conference on Language in Developing Countries. A section of Chapter VII is taken from my article 'Problems of a lingua franca: Swahili and the Trade Unions', *JAL*, 3, 3, 1964, 215–25, and again I am grateful to the editor, Dr Irvine Richardson, for permission to reproduce this.

To Dr John Iliffe of the University College, Dar es Salaam, I am grateful for his reading the manuscript, as I am also to my father. For the no less onerous task, that of typing the manuscript, my thanks are due to Valerie Green.

Finally, I must acknowledge my debt to H. E. Lambert and

Shaaban Robert, to whom I dedicate the book. From the former I learned something of the humility of the scholar; from the latter, one of my teachers, I learned of the richness and beauty of the language of which I am a student. From both I came to know something of what is meant by service to an ideal.

I · Language and Literature

The following words were given me by some sailors attached to an Arab boat, who called themselves Sowauli, which appears to be quite a distinct people from the Somauli. This tribe dwells on the Eastern Coast of Africa, extending from Mugdasho . . . to the neighbourhood of Mombasa. . . . These men possessed no knowledge of the interior country or tribes, having early been engaged in a sea-faring life, but mentioned that to the south of them were found tribes of Galla. Their language appears scarcely to deserve the name of a distinct dialect, but is a kind of mixed jargon, nearly allied to the Monjou, spoken at the sea ports. . . .

HENRY SALT, *A Voyage to Abyssinia and Travels*,
London, 1814, App. I

More than one hundred and fifty years have passed since Henry Salt recorded his impressions of the Swahili sailors he met on his voyage, from whom he noted down some samples of this coastal language, little known to Europe at the time. Since then Swahili has become the most widely known, taught, discussed, and spoken African language on the Continent and the national language of the United Republic of Tanzania. Whatever the future holds for it, the remarkable expansion and development of Swahili over the past hundred years constitute a most exciting chapter in a long history.

Salt can be forgiven for his mistaken assumptions about the language; sailors are notoriously bad ambassadors, and he himself was no more than superficially interested. But even if it were true at the time that 'the Swahili' were restricted to the coast, within a very few years the expansion of trade into the East African interior was to carry the language with it, right across the eastern part of Africa into what was to become the Belgian Congo, so that before the century closed Swahili was

1

being spoken on the coast between Brava in the north and Mozambique in the south: as far west as Elizabethville in the south and Stanleyville in the north. Indeed, within fifty years the missionary Ludwig Krapf could recommend to his readers,

> Now if we reflect that the Kisuaheli is spoken, at least under-stood from the Equator down to the Portuguese settlements at Mozambique, consequently, that . . . it offers the key to the language of the Interior, with which it is intimately related, we cannot help attaching great importance to this language. The scientific traveller who intends to collect informations on the coast, or to make researches in the Interior, can hardly proceed without the knowledge of this language. Nor can the merchant, who has an establishment on any part of this coast, conduct his mercantile transactions with a set of people, who are almost unmanageable, if the foreigner cannot converse with them in their own language without the pick-lock of a selfish interpreter.[1]

What Salt did not know was that at the time of his voyage there already had existed for many years a sophisticated verse literature in the language, centred on and around the island of Faza, off the northern Kenya coast. This literature, which drew its strength and inspiration from Islam, was already expanding southwards and was soon to produce its first nationalist poet in the person of Muyaka bin Haji.

Yet it is certainly true that the early history of Swahili, as we know it, belongs to the coast, the word itself being derived from the Arabic word for 'coasts' or perhaps 'port-towns'. Those who spoke it there have probably never been numerous; what has been startling, since the last century, has been the vast expan-sion in the numbers of those who acquired it as a second or third language.[2] Estimates of the numbers of those who now speak it are legion, varying from five to fifty million, but such estimates are the result of more or less inspired guesswork. What does it mean to say someone 'speaks' a language? He may speak it only on rare occasions; have control over a very limited vocabulary or range of structures; be able to speak it but deny that he can; may say he speaks it but does not in fact. Nevertheless, in default of precise figures and bearing the above warning in mind, one more estimate may be useful. We should recognize at least four main groups of speakers: first, those who speak Swahili as a 'mother' tongue, who probably do not number more than a million and who live mainly along the East African littoral, on the offshore islands of Zanzibar, Pemba, Mafia, the Comoros, and in a number of inland towns. These Swahili pools were left behind when the tide of Arab trade receded in the nineteenth century; places like Tabora, Ujiji, Bujumbura, as well as isolated trading settlements in Zambia and along the Congo river. Second, those who acquire it as a second language and use it for much of their daily life. There are certainly in excess of ten million in this group, living in the United Republic of Tanzania and in the Bantu-speaking areas of Kenya. Third, a group, probably in excess of a million who regularly use the language to a limited extent. This group is located in Uganda, the Nilotic-speaking areas of Kenya, and parts of the Congo-Kinshasa. Finally, there are those with a very limited control of the language who use it only sporadically. They are mainly located along the periphery of the main Swahili-speaking areas, in southern Somalia, northern Mozambique, parts of Rwanda, Burundi, and the western areas of the Congo around Kinshasa, the capital.

People often ask, when learning of the vast area over which Swahili is spoken, whether the same form of the language is spoken throughout. This is a difficult question in this form, but part of the answer can be provided by saying that a speaker of standard Swahili will probably be understood over the whole of the Swahili-speaking area. But here it must be pointed out that a standard form of the language did not exist until the second quarter of this century. Previous to that date the term Swahili referred primarily to a geographical area not to a linguistic nor to an ethnic unit. Linguistically we are dealing with a number of dialect clusters: some of the dialects like Chi-Miini,[3] spoken at Brava in Somalia, or Ki-Hadimu, spoken in southern Zanzibar, would be – as they are today – unintelligible to one another and to members of other clusters. That there was an immanent linguistic unity could be demonstrated by the linguist for all these dialects, but for the communities themselves, often separated from one another by other Bantu speakers, any such unity was probably comprehended only in the most general terms.

At the present time three major coastal dialect clusters can be recognized: a northern, central, and southern. The northern cluster comprises the dialects of the communities living around Lamu and Pate on the northern coasts of Kenya (Ki-Amu, Ki-Shela, Ki-Pate, Ki-Siu), together with that of the Bajun (Ki-Tikuu), who stretch northwards into Somalia. The above-mentioned dialect of Brava (Chi-Miini) is best regarded as a sub-group of this cluster.

The central cluster comprises the dialects of Vanga (Ki-Vumba) and Mtang'ata (Ki-Mtang'ata),[4] located on the southern Kenya and northern Tanzanian coasts respectively. To these must be added the various dialects of Pemba, and the two major rural dialects of Zanzibar (Ki-Tumbatu and Ki-Hadimu).

The southern cluster comprises the dialects of the Tanzanian coast south of Bagamoyo, including the island of Mafia, and the dialect of Zanzibar town, which was subsequently chosen to be the 'Standard' form of the language. To these must be added the 'bridge' dialects in and around Mombasa (Ki-Mvita, Chi-Jomvu, Ki-Ngare, with Chi-Chifundi farther to the south), which share some northern and some central features. The dialects of the Comoro Islands, however, require separate grouping (Ki-Nzwani, Shi-Ngazija).

These are the main coastal dialects, acquired as first languages by their speakers, even though they may use the Standard form as their primary language. The spread of

Swahili-speaking traders into the interior and the subsequent need for a lingua franca in areas – like the towns – of great linguistic diversity has led to the emergence of a number of up-country dialects, acquired as second or third languages. Most important of these are those spoken in parts of the eastern Congo and known collectively as Ki-Ngwana. Scarcely less important but much less well documented are the varieties which have developed as a result of contact with Asian and European settlers (Ki-Hindi and Ki-Settla). Some years ago a light-hearted caricature of the latter was made by J. W.,[5] and his examples would seem quite incredible to anyone unfamiliar with the rich, ringing tones of the Colonial *memsahib*. He comments, 'Kisettla or "mimi-kupiga-wewe" Swahili is believed to be derived from Kiswahili or "watu-wale-wawili-walipokuja" Swahili', and locates it thus, 'Kisettla is found in its purest form where coffee and wheat flourish in preference to coconuts, sweet potatoes or wimbe. . . .' Its grammar is attenuated: verbs are 'found in infinitive, imperative and first person singular, present indicative only' and its vocabulary is liberally sprinkled with English words 'Tia scones ndani oven and lete chai pot'. Ignorance is usually assisted by imagination, 'Lete kitu kama ndizi only round!'[6] Ki-Hindi also has its idiosyncrasies. An example is provided by Juma Aley in an essay entitled 'How the Different Races in Zanzibar Speak Swahili'. The story concerns a Goan, and hinges on the well-known Goan predilection for hot foods! On returning from his office he asked his servant if the curry was ready; on being told that it was, he asked, 'Pilipili gapi wewe tia? Nimetia kumi bwana! Sababu kidogo hii namna? Nani mambia? Kanambia bibi! Nani bibi bele yangu? Bibi kupa musahara wewe? Tia ishrini zaidi, mara ya pili mimi fukuza wewe!' (How many peppers did you put in? I put in ten, sir! Why so few? Who told you? Your wife told me! Who is she over me? Does she pay you? Put in twenty more, next time I'll sack you!) Such stories need not be taken too seriously, but the varieties of the language which they epitomize, coupled with their occurrence in the social context of master/servant relationships, did much to colour emotional attitudes to the language.

Even less is known about the varieties of Swahili which have grown up in towns as a result of the contact between Africans speaking diverse first languages. The recognition of a Standard form of the written language by 1930, and its subsequent propagation, has naturally affected the dialects, but it would be wrong to imagine that they all disappeared overnight. Mainland dialects, lacking the insulation enjoyed by those on the islands have suffered most, but it is difficult to generalize. More specifically those spoken by a small number of speakers, exposed to the eroding effects of Standard forms through education, local government, proximity to towns or lines of communication, appear to have lost most ground. Chi-Jomvu and Ki-Ngare, just outside Mombasa, and Ki-Mtang'ata around Tongoni, to the south of Tanga, seem definitely to be used regularly only by the older generation. Furthermore, working in south-eastern Pemba in 1957, I noticed that dialectal forms occurred far more frequently in villages in which a motor road had only recently arrived than in those which had been served by a road for a year or two. At the same time, however, the dialects of Pemba, rural Zanzibar, and Vumba were all found to be flourishing, despite the depressing account given of the Hadimu by Alice Werner in 1915:

> They inhabit the interior villages of the island, as fishermen and cultivators, and had, till recently, a distinct language of their own. This, however, is nearly forgotten, and it was only with great difficulty and after many disappointments that Miss Dora Abdy . . . succeeded in obtaining the sub-joined vocabulary. . . .[7]

Nor do the dialects of northern Kenya appear to be in any great danger. Nevertheless, it is reasonable to expect that with the passage of time the areas – both social and geographical – over which the dialects are spoken will shrink, but unless the Standard form of the language comes to be regarded as an acceptable substitute on all occasions, it is unlikely that they will disappear.

The picture at the present time is thus one of a 'Standard' form of the language being acquired as a second or third language by a large majority of speakers over a wide area of eastern Africa. Simultaneously there exist pockets of dialects spoken along the littoral and on the offshore islands mainly as a first language. Finally, there are a number of up-country dialects acquired as a second, third, or even fourth language and used as a means of communication between African and Asian or European, or between African and African, particularly in the towns where speakers of dozens of Bantu and Nilotic languages all seek a common means of communication. We cannot say with certainty which dialects existed at any particular historical period, nor, as a matter of fact, do we have adequate documentation on the present-day situation, but we do know that the earliest manuscript of a Swahili poem, from the first half of the eighteenth century, was written – in the Arabic script – in one of the northern dialects. Indeed, we can go further, and say that it seems on present evidence that the verse tradition of Swahili, as I shall discuss later, began and developed on and around the offshore islands of Lamu and Faza. From there it spread southwards at the beginning of the nineteenth century to Mombasa and thence across to Pemba, where a vigorous tradition of 'social' verse was soon established. None of the coastal dialects, apart from those of the northern cluster, Ki-Mvita and Ki-Pemba, seems to have supported a literature, at least until the very end of the nineteenth century.

Europeans who have come into contact with the language in one or other of its forms have not been slow to express opinions on it, with an authority often matched by an ignorance as great as their predecessor Henry Salt. It is not difficult to find views put forward that Swahili is somehow a hybrid of Arabic and a

Bantu language, that it is somehow not a 'proper' language,
that it has 'no grammar' nor literature. In 1952 we find a
reputable novelist declaring in one of those characteristically
cosy after-dinner speeches that Swahili was a '. . . "lingual
obscenity" to which no Briton "worth his salt" should be a
party',[8] and as recently as 1967, Susan Fuller writes in the
Times Educational Supplement of 24 February that: 'The long
association between the Bantus and Arabs in Zanzibar produced
Swahili.' It must be clearly stated that Swahili is a Bantu
language, one of several hundreds of such spoken across the
southern half of Africa. Over the centuries its coastal habitat
has brought it into contact with Arab, Portuguese, Indian,
British, and German traders and colonizers, so that its lexicon,
like that of English, has been enriched by many hundreds of
loan-words. By far the largest contribution comes from Arabic,
but English is rapidly catching up: the contribution from
Portuguese is, by comparison, meagre, a mere handful of words,
e.g. *meza*, table; *parafujo*, screw; *karata*, playing card; *gereza*,
prison; *nanasi*, pineapple. The contribution from Indian languages is less well established, but includes such words as *pesa*,
money; *gari*, vehicle; *embe*, mango; *limau*, lemon; *bangi*.
Indian hemp. Just as there have been fashions in English,
favouring words of French rather than of Anglo-Saxon origin,
so there have been times when words of Arabic origin have been
in favour, especially in Zanzibar and Mombasa. It was not
enough, then, merely to use the Arabic word, it was necessary
to attempt to pronounce it in an Arabic manner, to distinguish
'emphatic' from 'non-emphatic' consonants. However, here
there is something more than fashion at work; as the language
of Islam, the religion of the coast, Arabic enjoyed a quite special
status. Prior to the introduction of a Western type of secular
education, being educated meant learning to recite the Koran
and to write in an Arabic script. Small wonder that so much of
the vocabulary of coastal culture should be derived from
Arabic. In recent times English words have enjoyed a vogue,

particularly in the field of technology, where there are serious deficiencies in Swahili. More recently still, in the wake of nationalist fervour, words from other Bantu languages, too, have found favour. In Tanzania the National Assembly is referred to as the 'Bunge', which seems to have come from the language of the Ha, south-west of Lake Victoria. The State House, residence of the President, is referred to by some as 'Ikulu', which again comes from one of the up-country languages, possibly Gogo, or Nyamwezi.

During these last hundred years Swahili has meant many things to many people. It has provoked lifelong devotion as well as bitter hostility, from men and women of great sincerity. It has produced its crop of cranks, its irrational antagonists and sentimental devotees, as well as its notable scholars. You may study it at universities in the United States, the Soviet Union, India, and Japan, as well as in many countries in Western Europe. At a recent reception in Dar es Salaam I was able, thanks to Swahili, to enjoy a conversation with the Cuban Ambassador, which was then translated into Spanish for the benefit of his wife.

To the early administrators, bewildered by East Africa's diversity and multiplicity of languages – more than two hundred of them – Swahili appeared as a godsend. To those educationists who saw Swahili as a bar to the acquisition of a wider education based on English, Swahili was anathema. Consider, for example, the views of the Study Group who visited East and Central Africa in 1951–2 under the auspices of the Nuffield Foundation:

> We suggest, therefore, that because the present teaching of Swahili stands in the way of the strong development of both vernacular and English teaching, a policy should be followed which leads to its eventual elimination from all schools where it is taught as a *lingua franca*.[9]

and this view was expressed more forcibly by the East Africa Royal Commission of 1953–5:

We regard the teaching of Swahili as a second language to children whose early education has been in other vernaculars as a complete waste of time and effort.[10]

The debate has been going on a long time, and nowhere has it been keener than among writers. I shall come back to the issue in a later chapter, but it is worth citing one example from each side. Consider first the view of the novelist Joyce Cary:

But language is the very root of education, even at school; and after school, it is almost the whole of that greater education which continues throughout a man's life. It is by conversation, thought and reading, that he learns. For many great men books have been the only university. Suppose such men had been confined to Swahili or Hausa, how many books would they have read, and how much would they have learnt?[11]

Then compare this with the view of Shaaban Robert, the most notable literary figure to have appeared on the Swahili scene this century. My own translation does scant justice to the elegance of the original verse:

Swahili is rich, in its elegance and its proverbs; and I think that in the near future, it will be possible to translate many fields of education; and render a service to mankind both with insight and beauty; mother's breast is sweetest, no other satisfies.[12]

In the political field also Swahili has been near the centre of controversy: to politicians of the fifties it offered a means of unification:

It has proved our greatest asset in our pre-independence struggle as the instrument of uniting the people of the nation's different tribes.[13]

But this has not always been the case:

I feel, however, that it is my duty to add here in conclusion, that it is quite unnecessary to adopt the Ki-Swahili language as the Official Native Language in Buganda, and I am entirely opposed to any arrangement which would in any way facilitate the ultimate adoption of this language as the Official Native Language of the Baganda in place of, or at the expense of, their own language, since I feel convinced that such a course will assuredly bring about the loss of our tribal status and nationality among the Native tribes of Africa. . . .[14]

Even in the religious field, Swahili was not without its opponents. The early missionaries of the Church Missionary Society and the Universities' Mission to Central Africa quickly recognized the importance and value of the language as a means of propagating the Gospel, and it was from these two bodies that a number of the early scholars of Swahili came. But the early German Lutherans who moved into south-western Tanganyika believed otherwise and, in the words of Marcia Wright, believed that:

The African must be reached first emotionally, through his tribal existence. After becoming a Christian he would want to work as an expression of his new life, 'ora et labora'. Tribal languages were the key to this evangelism and the enemies were the detribalizing influences and subversive religious ideas tied up with Swahili.[15]

A similar attitude was held by the Anglicans in Uganda in the late twenties and early thirties, culminating in the preparation of a Memorandum from the Bishops of Uganda in which the use of Luganda as a lingua franca for Uganda was advocated.

By far the greatest part of this controversy was carried on in English by Europeans for other Europeans to support or deny. Whatever views Africans held on this matter, they were, with occasional exceptions, such as the example cited of the Kabaka, unpublished. One scans the Swahili Press of the German period, and of the twenties and thirties in vain. When there is discussion of some point in Swahili it is more often than not connected with the correctness or otherwise of some word or phrase. Yet, from my discussions with Africans, opposition there undoubtedly was to the use of Swahili in education, particularly from those areas where there existed strong ties to a local language, e.g. among the Luo and Kikuyu in Kenya and among Chaga and Haya in Tanganyika. In this connection, it is interesting to note the case of the Chaga in the early fifties, when, after the election of a Paramount Chief, the need for a 'national' language was felt. Unfortunately no one could decide on which of the constituent Chaga dialects should be selected, and ultimately they had to fall back on Swahili. And herein lay Swahili's strength; what was loved by none could be tolerated by all!

From the foregoing discussion it will be realized that, during the hundred years prior to Independence, the three most important factors affecting the official use of Swahili – and indirectly also its unofficial use – have been the attitudes of administrators, educators, and missionaries. But while vagaries of policy have contributed to important shifts in its popularity, its overall importance in many walks of life has been a sufficient and continuing incentive for a small but increasing group of European scholars to provide a documentation which, by now, is unequalled by that for any other African language. There are grammars for students of all levels of sophistication, including some specially written for colonists, missionaries, soldiers, and even postmen. There are grammars in Flemish, French, German, Gujarati, Italian, Russian, Swedish, and English; and dictionaries or word-lists in French, German, Italian, Gujarati, Russian, and English. The quality of this documentation is very uneven, the body of high scholarship is small, and virtually all of it is written for fellow Europeans, so that East Africans may ruefully reflect on the small effect all this material has had on the overall place of Swahili within, say, the educational system of East Africa. But the net result has been the accumulation of a vast body of knowledge about the language which East Africans can now join in augmenting, adapting, and refining. It is worth remembering that the desire to learn another's language springs only very rarely from a disinterested wish to communicate with one's fellow humans, so that while one may be out of sympathy with the motive, one may be grateful for the product. Let us accept the body of material which is now available and go on from there.

The impetus for German studies derived from their colonial interest in German East Africa, so that the bulk of their work dates from the period before 1917, though scholars in Germany have continued to work on earlier material collected. To the missionary J. L. Krapf we owe the first systematic grammar of the language (1850), and this was followed thirty years later by his monumental dictionary (1882), which has recently been reprinted. But Krapf, too, directed our attention to a body of verse in Swahili, sending back to Germany manuscripts in the Arabic script which engaged the attention of later generations of scholars. His fellow countrymen, Velten, Delius, Büttner, Seidel, and later Meinhof, built on these foundations, providing at the same time a wealth of reading material. Particularly useful collections – of value to historians and anthropologists as well as to students of language – were made by Velten and Büttner, and they were followed by E. Dammann, whose formidable contribution to the study of the literature has spanned the last thirty years or more.

French work was centred on the Holy Ghost Mission in Zanzibar and Morogoro. It was from Zanzibar that Fr. Charles Sacleux established his reputation, with studies of Swahili grammar and its dialects (both in 1909), but though the latter work remains unsuperseded until now, it is probably for his massive dictionary (1939–41) that he will be best remembered, a dictionary in which there is a wealth of dialectal and verse material not available elsewhere.

WINGATE COLLEGE LIBRARY
WINGATE N. C

Italian, Swedish, and to a lesser extent Belgian, interest has also been largely mission inspired. There are Italian Consolata Missions in southern Tanzania and in Kenya, and Passionist Fathers in central Tanzania, and it is from a Consolata father that a Swahili grammar (1953) and dictionary (1964) have recently appeared, written by Fr. Pick, who had earlier written a Kikuyu grammar. Swedish Missions are located in western Tanzania, in Burundi, and Rwanda, but there are also Lutherans around Dar es Salaam. On the other hand, there has been something of an upsurge of more secular interest from Scandinavians, and it is perhaps in part due to this that Courses were started in Uppsala in 1963, stimulating an elementary grammar to appear in the same year. Belgian studies go much further back to the beginning of the century, and there has been a steady trickle of works, from Whitehead's in 1928 to that of Natalis in the early sixties. India has only recently inaugurated the teaching of Swahili in Delhi, with a one-year Course in 1955, and plans for extending this to a two-year Diploma Course were approved in 1965; grammars and dictionaries exist in Gujarati, but these were produced locally in East Africa, and nothing has so far appeared from India. Japan has also initiated courses in the language, but few details are as yet available.

Soviet and East European interest in Swahili – excepting East Germany – dates mainly from the post-1945 period and is exclusively secular. All of the students working in Eastern Europe have suffered from a lack of opportunity, perhaps even inclination, to carry out empirical investigation of the problems in which they are interested, as well as from a lack of access to already published materials. Notwithstanding this handicap, a number of notable studies have already appeared, starting with the *Swahili–Russian, Russian–Swahili Dictionary* (1961?) of the doyen of Soviet African studies, Prof. D. A. Olderogge of Leningrad. Since then his colleagues and students from Leningrad and Moscow have made several studies of Swahili phonology, morphology, and syntax, among the most important being the work of A. I. Koutuzov, P. S. Kouznetzov, E. N. Miachina, V. M. Misiugin, N. V. Okhotina, and I. P. Yakovleva. From Czechoslovakia must be mentioned the work of K. F. Růžička. In contrast to this research, Chinese work in Swahili has concentrated on the teaching of operational skills to Chinese and on a programme of translations. The teaching programmes appear to be both intensive and extended, and some of the Chinese at present in Tanzania have reached a very high level of operational competence, certainly comparable with that of their Colonialist predecessors, and considerably more sophisticated than that of most other nationals whose performance is usually restricted to the most elementary levels. Virtually all the publications are of two kinds: political tracts and children's books. The former contain selections of the sayings of Chairman Mao and various other anti-Colonialist pamphlets; the latter include Chinese folk-tales, and are well produced, often beautifully illustrated and invariably cheap.

British contributions to Swahili studies start with Bishop Edward Steere's *Handbook of Swahili* (1870), which, with his *Exercises* (1878), formed the basis of initiation into the language for several generations of students, especially since it was revised successively by Madan (1894) and Hellier (*Exercises* 1934, and *Handbook* 1950). Steere was followed by his fellow missionaries Madan and Taylor, and while with increasingly heavy administrative responsibilities the focus of Swahili studies was soon to shift to the University of London, the mission component in those studies was an extremely important element at least until the end of the first half of the present century. Shortly after the turn of the century there appeared the first of a series of grammatical studies by distinguished women scholars, most of them owing some allegiance at some time or other to the Missions. First, Mrs Burt with her study of the Mombasa dialect (1910), then the Misses Werner, drawing on the first ten years' work at the School of Oriental Studies

(1927). This was followed in 1944 by Mrs Ashton's authoritative *Swahili Grammar* which remains the standard reference work. The author, now in her nineties, is indisputably the doyenne of British Swahili studies. Finally, Miss D. V. Perrott's *Teach Yourself Swahili* (1951), which many have found a most acceptable appetizer and introduction to Ashton. The feminine tradition in British Swahili studies is by no means dead, being most worthily upheld at the School of Oriental and African Studies by Miss M. A. Bryan and Miss J. Maw. To draw attention to this tradition is not to disparage the male contribution; administrator, educator, missionary, their names come quickly to mind: Broomfield, Allen, Bull, Snoxall, Lambert, Hollingsworth, Haddon, and the Secretaries of the Inter-Territorial Language (Swahili) Committee, Frederick Johnson and B. J. Ratcliffe. Johnson's name will probably always be linked with the *Standard Swahili–English, English–Swahili Dictionary*, which built on Madan's work of the early years of the century. Unhappily Johnson did not live to see his work appear in print, but at the time of its publication (1939) the dictionary was one of the most comprehensive available for any Bantu language and served as a model for others. No dictionary can, in the nature of things, be more than a temporary account of current usage, and nowhere is this truer than in the case of the modern languages of Africa receptive to so many technological changes. However, all future dictionary builders will owe a formidable debt to Madan and Johnson – as to Krapf and Sacleux – for their pioneering studies. More than twenty years have elapsed since Mrs Ashton wrote her *Grammar* and nearly thirty since the *Standard Dictionary* appeared: the time is ripe for a new leap forward, both in grammatical and lexical studies.

The most remarkable expansion of Swahili studies in recent years has been in the United States: true this has derived largely from America's confrontation with the Soviet Union and has been made possible by generous grants under the National Defence Education Act, but Swahili studies have been the richer for it. Courses are now offered at many Universities, from Columbia in the east to Los Angeles in the west and Texas in the south, and the Foreign Service Course is probably the most intensive Swahili Course anywhere, with the possible exception of Courses in China. In some cases British and European specialists have been responsible for running these Courses, Harries at Wisconsin; Snoxall at Los Angeles; Polomé at Texas, and Brain in Syracuse, but this is surely only a temporary phenomenon: young American scholars are emerging in increasing numbers, maintaining, as it happens, the feminine tradition: Carol Eastman, Judith Olinick, Ray Moses, and Carol Scotton have all recently completed Ph.Ds on various aspects of Swahili grammar and are themselves now teaching.

At this point it is worth considering some of the differences between the British and American approaches to Swahili. The most important of these is that whereas the British approach has almost always been aimed at giving the student operational competence – and many administrative officers reached a very high level of competence – the Americans have consistently given more weight to analysis. This is mainly due to the fact that the expansion of Swahili studies has taken place at the same time as an expansion in linguistic studies generally, and many of those now studying and teaching the language have received training in linguistics.

When Dr Krapf sent back to Germany some samples of Swahili verse in the Arabic script he opened up for Western scholarship a new field of research, which his countrymen and their British and European colleagues were to till with distinction – Büttner, Dammann, Sacleux, Taylor, Werner, Hichens, Allen, Harries, Lambert, and Knappert. Some, mainly collectors, others, mainly editors. Yet in honouring such scholars, we must stress their debts to Swahili colleagues: that of Taylor to Mohammed Sikujua, of Hichens to Sir Mbarak Ali Hinawy, and of Allen to the el-Buhry family. Time will accord final judgement on the merit of their contributions, but as a result of their labours it is now possible for students everywhere to discern something of the variety and content of the Swahili verse tradition, to assess its achievements and honour its poets.

One cannot say when, nor, really, with whom, that tradition first developed, but the oldest known manuscript, preserved in Hamburg, is dated 1728. Since the language and style of this poem do not suggest an inchoate art, one may with some confidence place the earliest developments before the eighteenth century; indeed, in the opinion of Dr J. Knappert the language of the oldest known poem, the *Hamziya*, 'is so archaic that it cannot be dated later than the seventeenth century'.[16] The early poets seem to have lived and worked on the northern coast of Kenya, perhaps in and around Pate, writing religious and didactic verse in the Arabic script and using one of the northern dialects of Swahili. Their inspiration was Islam, and Islamic culture and thought impregnate all the early verse. Indeed, in Dr Knappert's opinion, 'Swahili culture is essentially Oriental, not African in its material as well as in its spiritual aspects',[17] and he goes on, 'In this Swahili culture it is very difficult to find indisputably African features.' The most common form of this verse was the *utendi* (*utenzi*),[18] the long narrative poem which commonly dealt with the wars of the faithful, the lives of saints or heroes, in short the subject matter of an epic literature. Regarding the origins of these *tendi*, Dr L. Harries considers that 'there can be no doubt that the Swahili *tendi* derived from the Maghazi legendary literature . . . Arabian narratives, mostly in rhymed prose . . . consisting of legendary accounts based on a modicum of historical facts dealing with the wars of the Prophet Mohammed after the Hijra'.[19]

As yet we know little about the manner in which such poems were recited, but it is probable, if current performance is anything to go by, that they were intoned or chanted. Nor do we know much about the occasions on which recitation took place, but again, it seems not unreasonable to suppose that their religious content fitted them for many solemn occasions. However, an important lacuna in our knowledge here is the fact that we know so little about the form of the society for which such poems were recited: Dr Knappert is probably right to assert that, 'This literature has function in the daily life of the Swahili as it is often quoted, and recited on special occasions',[20] but until we know who 'the Swahili' are we shall not be much wiser, and even then certainly not in a position to assume that it was for communities of this kind that the verse of the eighteenth century was composed. These long narrative poems can be divided into verse units of thirty-two syllables, in which the eighth, sixteenth, and twenty-fourth syllables (usually consonant plus vowel) all rhyme. The final syllable of the verse, the thirty-second, rhymes with all other such throughout the poem. Consider the following verse from the *Utenzi wa Mikidadi na Mayasa*:

> 'Mayasa ali mzu*ri*, na weupe wa fakha*ri*, na uso wake mdawa*ri*, haiba na ushujaa'

Translation is a difficult art, especially when one has to take account of a particular metrical pattern as well as of an accentual system which cannot be known with certainty because one is not sure of the relation between the patterns of speech and those of chant. If this verse were spoken, then a strong beat would fall on the syllable preceding the rhyme and weaker beats on the penultimate syllable of each word of two syllables or more. In the following translation I have retained only the metrical structure:

> And the beautiful Mayasa, was fair indeed to look upon, full faced she was her visage shone, with courage and serenity.

By the beginning of the nineteenth century the poetic tradition was moving south, to Mombasa, where the first nationalist poet, Muyaka bin Haji al-Ghassaniy, lived and worked. He is

accredited with having brought to perfection the other main
form of Swahili verse, the quatrain (*shairi* pl. *mashairi*). Here
there is much greater metrical freedom, but the verse usually
comprises sixty-four syllables, divided into four lines of sixteen
syllables each. The first three lines all have medial rhymes at
the eighth syllable, as well as terminal rhymes. The entire
fourth line may recur throughout the poem, or it may have a
medial rhyme like the three previous lines. The name quatrain
suggests that the poem as a whole has only a single four-line
verse, and there are many cases where this is so. Equally
common, however, are poems with several verses, though even
here it is considered a mark of distinction if each of the verses
expresses some complete thought. The themes of such verses
cover a wide range; particularly popular is that perennially
absorbing topic, man's relationship to woman:

> Risala alipoku*ja*, na maneno kunambia
> Nalikaa kukungo*ja*, nawe hukunitokea
> Likupeteni, mmbe*ja*? Lililo kukuzuia?
> Leo wanitenda haya – kesho utanitendaje?[21] (Muyaka)

(When the messenger came, and told me the news, I was
sitting waiting for you, and you didn't appear, what hap-
pened to you, gorgeous? What kept you away? Today you
do this to me – what will you do to me tomorrow?)

Muyaka is also attributed with the composition of a number
of fiercely patriotic verses, inciting his fellow Mombasans to rise
up against the overlordship of Seyyid Said, Sultan of Oman, and
I shall give an example in Chapter III.

Whether or not Muyaka was the first Swahili poet to use his
art for political purposes, his example has been followed by
many right up to the present day. Indeed, I think that political
and social satire constitute an important part of the corpus of
'shairi' poetry. In the early 1870s, for example, following
Seyyid Barghash's accession to the Sultanate in Zanzibar, the

Mazrui leader Sh. Mbaruk bin Rashid demonstrated his independence from Omani jurisdiction by extensive raids on the villages along the Kenya coast. The acting Governor of Mombasa, appointed by the Sultan, Muhammed bin Abdullah, made many efforts to catch the rebel, who, on more than one occasion, was forewarned by his friend the poet, Suud bin Said al-Maamiry. In the oblique and allusive style characteristic of this genre the poet warned his friend and taunted the Governor. On one occasion, when a stratagem of Mohammed to bring back Sh. Mbaruk in chains had failed, the poet produced the following verses:

> Alipelekwa za poso nzuri
> Shali ya maua na deuli zari
> Mbura kuolewa kamwe hakukiri
>
> Kuowana siri siyo kiungwana
> Arusi nda tari kutezwa mtana
> Mbura adhihiri apate jivuna.[22]

(She was sent betrothal gifts, flowered shawls and scarves, embroidered with gold, but Mbura would not agree to marry him. Civilized folk don't marry in secret; the bride should be danced to during the afternoon, where she can be seen and show off her talents.)

Shortly afterwards, when Muhammed's Governorship was confirmed, Suud was arrested and jailed. The taunts of Suud remind one of the satires of Skelton in Tudor England, who, in his bitter attacks on Cardinal Wolsey, was often in danger of arrest, even if he himself was not actually jailed:

> Yet it is a wily mouse
> That can build his dwelling house
> Within the cattés ear,
> Withouten dread or fear.

> It is a nice reckoning
> To put all the governing,
> All the rules of this land
> Into one mannés hand.[23]

Sometimes the object of the Swahili poet's attack was a suitor, as in this example from Pemba:

> Nawaambia kwa yakini tena yangu yawapate
> Shume angia mjini atakhasiri mujute
> Hana moyo wa imani angiapo apafute
> Yuwaja mkongwe mate watoto mutahadhar[24]

(I'm telling you for certain, mind my words, there's a tom-cat coming to town, he'll ruin it and you'll be sorry; he's quite unscrupulous, wherever he enters he wipes out (its good name), there's a 'slaverer' (from the dripping jaws of tom-cats, jackals, etc.) coming, watch out you youngsters!)

Enough to put off any prospective father-in-law!

In the modern poetry, especially in newspapers, the allusions may be much less subtle, as in the following verses:

> Banda unafitinisha, kuwafiti jirani
> Wataka kugombanisha, au ni shabaha gani?
> Ili kuyahatarisha, maisha ya masikini?
>   Banda ni kiherehere, mara hili mara ile
>
> Mara Banda waropoka, hujuwi wasema nini
> Kwamba wa Nyasa mpaka, upitishwe ukingoni
> Hayo unayoyataka, sisi hatuyathamini
>   Kati na kati ya ziwa, ulimopita mpaka[25]

(Banda, you're making trouble, slandering your neighbour, do you want to provoke a fight, or what is your aim? Are you putting the lives of the poor in jeopardy? Banda's capricious, first one thing then another. Then he blathers, you don't know what he's saying, that the boundary of Nyasa should be made to pass along the (eastern) shore, we take no account of what you want, in the middle of the lake was where the boundary passed!)

From Mombasa the verse tradition spread to Pemba, where it flourished during the latter part of the nineteenth century and into the first decades of this. All the poets seem to have lived in or around the main centres and the clove-plantations and to have enjoyed the patronage of wealthy Arab land-owners. Here they acted as commentators of daily life, vying with one another in their efforts to record their feelings on such diverse topics as hunger, love, hardship, the spirits, politics, and notable people. One of the most famous of these poems describes the visit of Suleiman bin Nasor Lemky to Pemba and how, as the guests were preparing to settle down to a sumptuous feast, they were descended on by a swarm of bees:

> Mambo ya juzi Selemu, ama hayawasifiki
> Hicho ni kisa adhimu, wala mwerevu hacheki
> Waarabu mahashamu, vidudu kuwahariki
> Kumbe kukimbia nyuki, mashekhe mbio ni bora
>
> Ilitoka nyingi dhifa, jamii tukahanaki
> Kukirimiwa shurafa, vyakula kwa mishikaki
> Ikatutokea afa, yote tukayatariki
> Kumbe kukimbia nyuki, mashekhe mbio ni bora
>
> Vita vya nyuki vigumu, nakhiari vya bunduki
> Huja hawana salama, wala hawana sihiki
> Wakitokea karamu, kataan hailiki
> Kumbe kukimbia nyuki, mashekhe mbio ni bora.[26]

(The events of the other day, Selemu, are indescribable, a really serious matter, that no sensible man would laugh at, how some insects threw the Arab dignitaries into a panic, goodness when it comes to escaping from bees, my lord, flight is the answer.

There was a magnificent feast, everyone was enjoying

C

themselves, distinguished guests were being entertained, roast meat was served. Danger descended on us and we took to our heels, goodness, when it comes to escaping from bees, my lords, flight is the answer.

Fighting bees is no joke, fighting with rifles is preferable, when they come you have no peace and they don't listen to reason, when they turn up there's no eating the feast, goodness . . .)

The poet then goes on to describe the antics of the various dignitaries in terms which long remained a source for much ribald comment.

By the end of the nineteenth century members of the el-Buhry family were writing *tenzi* from Tanga; Hemedi b. Abdulla b. Said el-Buhry describing the rebellion of Bushiri against the Germans and keeping alive the distinguished family tradition. If it is true that the main branches of the family came from Pemba and northern Kenya respectively, then we can say that there is little literature of value to be found south of Mombasa until German times – and this includes Zanzibar.

Of the literary tradition as a whole, certain things stand out: it derived its inspiration from Islam; appears to have existed symbiotically with Arab ruling dynasties and to have disseminated southwards from a single centre in northern Kenya. For its symbiosis with Arab ruling groups the evidence is chiefly the negative occurrence of any verse traditions among those coastal communities where some form of Arab overlordship was lacking. My own experience on Pemba was that as soon as one left the towns and the clove-plantations the verse disappeared. This was true also of Tongoni, and seems to have been true of Vumba, Chifundi, and even the Ngare and Jomvu dialects around Mombasa. Furthermore, with the exception of *tenzi* known to have been composed within the last hundred years, virtually all the 'classical' *tenzi* appear to have been composed and handed on in a northern dialect, even where locals claim, as they do on Pemba, that they reflect local usage. In this they differ markedly from the shorter quatrains which, again on Pemba, but also on the mainland, reflect local usage to a much greater extent. Yet there are many questions which remain unanswered: why did this tradition take root around Pate and Lamu, and not around any of the other Arab settlements from Mogadishu to Kilwa, which latter we know to have been a flourishing city-state in medieval times? Was there any special tradition associated with the ruling dynasty of Pate, the Nabhani, or has the evidence from earlier times disappeared? Again, why was Zanzibar so sterile while its northern neighbour, Pemba, was so fertile a ground for verse: was there anything in Mazrui traditions which the Busaidi dynasty in Zanzibar did not share? Or should one give greater weight to the social structure of the various African societies with which the Arabs co-existed? Answers to these questions must be sought from many specialists; the archaeologist, the historian, the student of comparative literature, the Islamist, and the linguist, but there is no certainty that such answers will be forthcoming, so shrouded in uncertainties is the early history of the coast in all but the most tentative outlines.

FURTHER READING

GENERAL

The best general ethnographic account of the area is A. H. J. Prins's:

> *The Swahili-speaking Peoples of Zanzibar and the East African Coast*, International African Institute, London, 1961, 2nd. ed. 1967.

and this author's more recent study of Lamu is a good introduction to these coastal communities:

> A. H. J. PRINS, *Sailing from Lamu*, van Gorcum, 1965.

The most useful general study of Islam in East Africa is provided by:

> J. SPENCER TRIMINGHAM, *Islam in East Africa*, Clarendon, 1964.

LANGUAGE

The journal *Swahili* is the only journal devoted entirely to Swahili studies. It appears twice a year and is published by the Institute of Swahili Research, University College, Dar es Salaam. It contains articles of historical, linguistic, and literary interest, and includes lists of new words and reviews.

The reader who wishes to find out something about how Swahili works might look at either of the following two books: the former will appeal to the linguistically unsophisticated, while the latter is more suitable for those with some linguistic training:

D. V. PERROTT, *Teach Yourself Swahili*, E.U.P., 1951.

E. C. POLOMÉ, *Swahili Language Handbook*, Centre for Applied Linguistics, 1967.

The student who wishes to go further should consult the select bibliography of works on Swahili language on pp. 141–45, which lists the most important works to date.

LITERATURE

The two most useful general works on this subject are:

LYNDON HARRIES, *Swahili Poetry*, Clarendon, 1962.

JAN KNAPPERT, *Traditional Swahili Poetry*, Leiden, 1967.

The former attempts to cover all the main genres of Swahili poetry, while the latter concentrates on the *utenzi* literature.

Both these authors have contributed widely to academic journals, but the following are perhaps the most generally helpful:

L. HARRIES, 'Popular Verse of the Swahili Tradition', *Africa*, Vol. XXXII, 1952, 158–64.

L. HARRIES, 'Cultural Verse-forms in Swahili', *African Studies*, Vol. XV/4, 1956, 176–87.

L. HARRIES, 'The Swahili Quatrain', *Afrika und übersee*, Vol. XLI, 1/2, 1957, 67–71.

JAN KNAPPERT, 'Notes on Swahili Literature', *ALS*, Vol. VII, 1966, 126–59.

JAN KNAPPERT, 'Some Aspects of Swahili Poetry', *Tanzania Notes*, 66, 1966, 163–70.

JAN KNAPPERT, 'Swahili Songs', *Afrika und übersee*, Vol. L, 1967, 163–72.

In addition, Lyndon Harries has recently edited a collection of the gnomic verse of Ahmad Nassir bin Juma Bhalo, *Poems from Kenya*, Wisconsin University Press, 1966.

An excellent example of an *utenzi* in the role of a social commentary is provided by the recent publication of *The Medicine Man: swifa ya Nguvumali*, Hasan bin Ismail, edited and translated by Peter Lienhardt, Clarendon, 1968.

The East African Literature Bureau (P.O. Box 30022, Nairobi) publishes a series of modern and traditional texts with translations, covering both prose and verse, under the title *Johari za Kiswahili*, which would serve as a good introduction to the tradition itself, though for the earlier verse more specialized studies must be consulted.

II · Early History

'Zanzibar is a large and splendid island, some 2,000 miles in circumference. The people are all idolaters. They have a king and a language of their own and pay tribute to none.   MARCO POLO
(*The Travels of Marco Polo*, R. E. Latham,
Penguin Books, 1958, p. 301)

Historians agree that by Zanzibar Marco Polo meant the whole of the East African coast, but what was the language? Swahili has as good a claim as any East African language and certainly better advocates, but what is the evidence for the existence of Swahili at that time? Mr S. E. Munisi, in a recent letter to *The Nationalist*, seems to think the case is proven (10 July 1967):

> Swahili is unique amongst the languages of Africa in having a written tradition dating back some centuries before the arrival of the Europeans. The Swahili words [*sic*] to be written appeared in the 10th century. It was a European scholar at the brilliant court of Roger II of Sicily, al-Idrisi (1100–1166) who was the first to note the ancient name of Zanzibar as Unguja. . . . He records the names of certain bananas in Swahili. Kikonde, mkono wa tembo, muriani and sukari. . . .[1]

The 'European' scholar in question wrote a work of geography in Arabic, the *Kitab Rujar*, of which no complete text has been published, but certain sections have been translated into French and Russian. Here are the relevant passages in Ferrand:

> Parmi les îles de Djāwaga comprises dans la présente section, on compte celle de Andjaba dont la ville principale

28

se nomme, dans la langue de Zanguebar, Ungūdya, et dont les
habitants, quoique mélangés, sont actuellement pour la
plupart musulmans . . . on s'y nourrit principalement de
bananes. Il y en a cinq espèces, savoir: les bananes dites
kundi, fīlī dont le poids s'élève quelquefois à douze onces;
'omānī, muriyānī, sukarī. . . .[2]

There is no reference here to Swahili, though in Standard
Swahili there are words *kikonde* and *kisukari* meaning types of
banana, and the *mkono wa tembo* of today may well refer to the
same type of banana that is mentioned by Idrisi. Sacleux suggests that the former is derived from *konde*, a cultivated field,[3]
while Dr Knappert has suggested to me that it has an Indonesian source. *Sukari* comes from Arabic. What we have, therefore, in an Arabic text, are a few words which can plausibly be
linked to present-day Swahili words. But this fact alone does
not enable us to say that at the time Swahili was being spoken;
these are, after all, loan words, and nothing is said about the
population who used them. Much more interesting in this respect is the word 'Unguja', because though no convincing
etymology has been proposed for it, it certainly looks like a
Bantu word, and it might be reasonable to suppose that people
who had a Bantu-like name for their locality also spoke a Bantu
language.

In this connection it is worth looking to see what the linguists can tell us about the early history of the Bantu languages.
Professor M. Guthrie, of the School of Oriental and African
Studies, has been working on a comparative study of the Bantu
languages for more than twenty years, carefully sifting
material for a large number of Bantu languages. As he suc-
cinctly puts it:

The raw material for any comparative study of languages is
the existence of groups of cognates from language to language, characterised by what are known as sound-shifts.[4]

It has proved possible to construct rather more than 2,000 sets of cognates from some 200 Bantu languages. From this data one can infer that all the members of a given set occur by virtue of the occurrence of an item in some 'proto'-language. This item is termed a root, and the members of the set are termed 'reflexes' of that root. Some of the roots appear to occur over the whole or a very large part of the Bantu field, and these are termed 'general' roots. There are more than 500 of these. The next stage involves the selection of a number of test languages, twenty-eight in all, and the working out of the percentage of general roots in each of these languages. The languages with the highest percentages, Bemba (54) and Luba-Katanga (50), turn out to form a nucleus in the centre of Africa, but both Kongo (44) and Swahili (44) on the west and east coasts respectively have a very high percentage of reflexes of general roots. From this evidence Professor Guthrie suggests that Proto-Bantu was spoken somewhere in the centre of the nucleus and attributes the progressive diminution from the nucleus to the dispersal northwards and southwards of ancestors of the present-day languages. The fact that Standard Swahili has a high percentage of general roots might be accounted for by assuming that these early speakers moved out from the nucleus to the east coast at a very early stage. We cannot put a date to such a movement, but since the general roots contain a root for forging iron, it may be presumed that the dispersal took place at some time subsequent to a knowledge of iron-working. The earliest Iron Age data so far obtained from anywhere in Africa south of the equator is from a site, within the nucleus area, in Zambia, for which the end of the first century A.D. is given by radio-carbon dating. In a recent article Professor Roland Oliver has suggested[5] that the first five centuries A.D. should be regarded as the dispersal period to the coasts, and remarks that while the *Periplus* of the first century made no reference to people who might be Bantu-speakers, the available accounts of Ptolemy, edited in fifth-century Alexandria, do refer to 'man-eating

Ethiopians' to the south, perhaps around Cape Delgado. There is, however, one important caveat: while Swahili has a high percentage of general roots, its nearest neighbours among the test languages are Sukuma (Tanzania) 41, Yao (data from Malawi) 35, and Bemba (within the nucleus in Zambia) 54. We would presumably have to modify our view of East African history as far as Swahili is concerned if it turned out that intervening languages had markedly different scores. It must be remembered that among the test languages there are eight from eastern Africa, of which three (Nyankore, Nyoro, and Ganda) are geographically contiguous in Uganda and two more (Kikuyu and Kamba) in Kenya. Apart from these languages, East Africa, with nearly 200 Bantu languages, is represented by only Sukuma and Yao.

On the present linguistic evidence, therefore, it is possible to argue that some form of Proto-Standard Swahili was being spoken on the coast before the tenth century. But the reports available to al-Idrisi of the types of banana eaten in Unguja did not, and perhaps could not, say anything very useful about the people who used such terms. Indeed, such information, were it available, might mislead us further, since the banana sellers in Dar es Salaam market today use a variety of terms which have far wider provenance than Swahili, and this raises another problem about the interpretation of various words found in texts. Because Swahili is a Bantu language, and therefore shares a large number of its roots with other Bantu languages, one cannot in most cases say unambiguously whether a particular Bantu-like root which has a reflex in current Swahili was in fact being used in a Swahili-milieu at the time. Words which are known to be loans, of course, complicate the matter still further. Finally, one must remember that these early words are embedded in Arabic texts in the Arabic script. Their interpretation, as we shall see below, is a matter for more or less inspired guess-work, and in all cases known to me the interpretations aim at producing words which are current in

Standard Swahili. If one were looking at a French manuscript of Norman times, for example, in which some English words were believed to occur, it would be unreasonable to expect them to look like modern English. Even supposing we knew what dialect we were dealing with, one would expect some form of sound-change to have occurred, especially since we are going much of the way back to the time of the hypothesized dispersal of the Bantu languages from a central nucleus. The comparative linguistic evidence does not take us very far.

The writer in *The Nationalist* quoted at the outset of this chapter mentioned also some Swahili words appearing in the tenth century, and it is worth while looking at the words to which he referred. They occur in the Arab geographer, al-Mas'udi's account of his travels to the East which has been translated by C. B. de Meynard and P. de Courteille. Three important words occur in the following passage:

> Pour en revenir aux Zendjes et à leur rois, le nom des rois de ce pays est *Waklimi*, ce que signifie fils du Seigneur suprême (p. 29) . . . Ils donnent à Dieu le nom de *Maklandjalou*, dont le sens est le souverain Maître (p. 30) . . . mais la base de leur alimentation est la dorrah et une plante appelée *kalari*, que l'on tire de terre comme la truffe (p. 30).[6]

The only published discussion of these terms occurs in Dr G. S. P. Freeman-Grenville's account of 'Medieval Evidence for Swahili',[7] where he suggests that they may be interpreted as 'wafalme', 'mkulu-ngulu', and 'kalala'. Any interpretation does, it seems to me, need to take a number of factors into account:

   a. the context in which the word occurs;
   b. the consonantal profile of the word in question;
   c. the possibility that the words may be in some dialectal form of Arabic;
   d. the possibility that unfamiliar words might well have been particularly prone to amendment by successive copyists;

   e. the possibility that proto-Swahili forms would be liable to exhibit differences in shape due to sound changes.

   f. variant readings.

Dr Freeman-Grenville's interpretation of Waklimi (and the various alternative readings) accords reasonably well with the context, but not so well with the profile. The early forms of 'mfalme', whose etymology has long been disputed, occur as '*mfalume/mfaume*', and Dr Knappert's suggestion of 'wakulima' is clearly more closely in accord with the consonantal profile, though quite unsuitable for the context. More recently he has suggested [7a] that it could be read as *iqlimi*, district head, but while this fits both profile and context, it is not clear whether the term was in use at that period with that designation. On the other hand, little attention has been given to the meaning 'fils du Seigneur suprême', which might support an interpretation of the 'wa' element as a possessive, and the 'kl/ql' element as yielding 'kulu', as is done with 'maklandjalou'.

   In accepting Wainwright's interpretation of '*mkulu-ngulu*', Freeman-Grenville adopts a transliteration *maliknajlu*, and the context is again better served than the profile, but this is not so for '*kalala*'. The *Standard Dictionary* defines this as the 'tough, leathery sheath of the coconut flower-stem', and Freeman-Grenville can only reconcile this with a 'plant which is dug up from the ground like truffles' by suggesting that the writer may have got the wrong word for the substance in question, since 'the top shoot of the coconut palm, which is delicious as a salad, might easily be mistaken at table for a root'. Here Knappert's suggestion of '*ki(l)azi*' clearly makes better sense if one accepts that the profile is susceptible of such an interpretation. But if we accept a meaning of 'sweet potato' here, where does this take us? Is the sweet potato indigenous to East Africa, if not, what do we know of its provenance? It would look, in this form at any rate, like a modern southern dialectal form, but it might well be an early loan. Furthermore, one must not rule out altogether the possibility that such words might be Arabic shapes, perhaps dialectal forms. The profile from which *maklandjalou* is obtained, for example, has an initial element suggestive of *mlk*, dominion, though Knappert is confident in this case that an interpretation *mukulu ijulu*, 'The great one above', is to be preferred.[7b] The reader will appreciate that the position is far from clear, and an examination of any manuscript of Mas'udi would well repay the effort involved.

The next important source of possible early Swahili words is the Arabic text of the history of Kilwa, which was probably composed during the early sixteenth century. The history relates that the first king of the land was Sultan Ali ibn al-Husain, surnamed *'Nguo nyingi'*, and that his son was known as *'mkoma watu'*. Later in the history there is reference to another Sultan, Talut ibn al-Husain, 'nicknamed *Hasha hazifiki*'.[8]

Once again a difficult problem of interpretation is raised: 'nguo nyingi' is certainly a plausible interpretation, especially in the light of the tradition that 'he encircled the island with clothing', but it is worth looking at Strong's vocalization *'Ighawamij'*,[9] which raises the possibility of some epithet like *'mkuu wa miji'*, similarly fairly plausible. One probably cannot accept the voiceless 'k' here, but there may well be a more acceptable alternative which retains the voiced sound. If one accepts *'mkoma watu'* as reasonable there are objections to Freeman-Grenville's explanation of this as 'the Borassus palm of the people', as I have pointed out elsewhere. The expression *'kukoma watu'* with the connotation of 'destroying or finishing people' occurs in poetry and seems not an unreasonable epithet for a king and not incompatible with the description of him as 'a goodly young man'. The words 'Hasha hazifiki' are extracted from the consonantal profile sh z f k, and while the pointing lends plausibility to the suggested vowels, there is nothing to suggest the 'h' nor the word division. One might equally have 'ashazifika', 'he arrived at them' (the twin cities of Mecca and Medina), though neither this nor Freeman-Grenville's suggestion of 'Nay, he'll not arrive at them' seems particularly felicitous. The fact is that on the evidence so far available one cannot place too much confidence on the interpretations. More importantly, however, one might reasonably ask, supposing that we were to accept this small collection of words as examples of some form of proto-Swahili, why do they give no evidence for sound-changes? Is Swahili somehow different from other languages, or is the time-scale somewhat shorter than we have hitherto supposed? Finally, there is no evidence of who spoke these words: the *History of Kilwa* is silent on the populations who might have used the nicknames we have cited, and while other groups are mentioned by travellers, no connection is made between the Swahili-like words and those who used them. Of the early travellers the Arab, Ibn Battuta, who visited East Africa in the fourteenth century, is one of the earliest to refer specifically to 'Swahili', but there is no evidence to support a view that he used the term in other than its geographical sense. He writes:

> Je m'embarquai sur la mer dans la ville de Makdachaou, me dirigeant vers le pays des Saouâhil (les rivages) et vers la ville de Couloua (Kiloua), dans le pays des Zendjs. Nous arrivâmes à Manbaça, grande île, à une distance de deux journées de navigation de la terre des Saouâhil . . . Ses habitants . . . ils ne se livrent pas à la culture, et on leur apporte des grains des Saouâhil.[10]

It is not clear from this account where the Swahili were located; it is presumably somewhere between Mombasa and Kilwa, or even between Mombasa and Mogadishu, but it is clearly somewhere within the 'country of the Zendjs'. Indeed, in view of Pemba's later reputation as a granary, it would not be unreasonable to locate it there. However, there is no reference to the community that organized this export trade either here or elsewhere. It has been pointed out that the Portuguese made no reference to the Swahili, though a number of tribes are mentioned by name, e.g. Segeju (Moceguejos, 1571), Zimba (1609), Makua (Macua, 1609), Samia (?) (Mozungulos, post-1594). This does not seem to me to be at all surprising, since the term Swahili is an Arabic one with a primarily geographical reference, and there is no obvious reason why the Portuguese should take this over when they had the term 'Moor' available. We read that Kilwa is a 'Moorish town. . . . It has a Moorish king over it. . . . Of the Moors there are some fair and some black. . . . These Moors speak Arabic and follow the creed of the Alcoran.'[11] Like Battuta, more than a century before him, Barbosa makes a simple contrast between these Moors and 'Heathen'. He comments of Angoya, to the south of Mozambique, 'The natives thereof are some black and some tawny, they go bare from the waist up. . . . They speak the native language of the country, that of the Heathen, but some speak Arabic.'[12] Father dos Santos, writing at the end of the sixteenth century, talks of 'Moors' and 'Cafres', but does not mention language.[13]

English comments from this period are rare, but where they do occur they substantiate the accounts of the Portuguese. Consider, for example, this description of Malindi at the beginning of the seventeenth century:

> Melinde is the name of a kingdome, and of the chiefe Citie thereof: the Inhabitants especially neere to the Sea are Moores, and build their houses after the manner of Europe. The women are white, and the men of colour inclining to white, notwithstanding the situation under the Line. They have black people also, which are Heathens for the most part.[14]

From about this period, too, comes an interesting word-list. The words certainly look like Swahili – and this would therefore rank as the first word-list of the language – but most of the words collected appear to be reflexes of the general roots I referred to earlier in this chapter, and could therefore have formed part of some other Bantu language. It was collected by one William Payton on a visit to the Comoro Islands in 1613, and is worth quoting in full:

> They speak a kind of Morisco Language which is somewhat difficult to learn, and our continuance there (was) short; so that I took only notice of these few words following, which are sufficient to call for victuals or fruits, when Portuguese language is wanting; and to speak to any of the country people, who understand not Portuguese, viz:

Gumbey,	a Bullock	(Ng'ombe)
Buze,	a Goat	(Mbuzi)
Coquo,	an Hen	(Kuku)
Tundah,	Oranges	(Tunda)
Demon,	Lemons	(Ndimu)
Mage,	Water	(Maji)
Surra,	a kind of drink	(Sura, Portuguese for the first juice of palm tree)
Quename,	a Pine	(?Kinamasi or Lami)
Seivoya,	Cocker nuts	
Figo,	Plantains	(Figo, Portuguese for fig)
Cartassa,	Paper	(Karatasi)
Sinzano,	a Needle	(Sindano)
Arembo,	Bracelets	(Urembo)
Soutan,	the King	(Sultani)[15]

More than a century later, in 1776, the Frenchman Morice makes a triple division between Arabs, Moors, and Africans. The Arabs are recent arrivals in the post-Portuguese period, while the Moors antedate the Portuguese. Indeed, when the Portuguese arrived in Kilwa 'they had to fight with the Moors and Africans who already, to all intents and purposes formed a single society among themselves'.[16] Morice relates how Moors and Africans had only gradually learned to co-exist and how 'The cunning and ingenuity of the Moors at length overcame the fear and distrust of the Africans and the two nations mixed

with each other by contracting marriages'.[17] There is no reference to any language called Swahili, but Freeman-Grenville
has noted one example of a reference to a 'Moorish' language,
and Morice specifically refers to his own inability to make himself understood with Africans to whose linguistic diversity he
also refers.[18] However, at about this time there is one interesting letter from a Prince Kombo, in which the writer refers to
another letter he has written in his 'national language'.[19] While
the original letter has been lost, and while no identification of
language is given, Swahili has a fair claim here; Prince Kombo
was, after all, a widely travelled man and had probably been
born and brought up on the coast.

But, in any case, by this time we have written evidence for
Swahili in the manuscript of *Utenzi wa Tambuka*, referred to in
the last chapter, written in a northern dialect, and from then
on the evidence is continuous. Until the last few months this
represented the earliest written evidence for Swahili. Recently,
however, Dr E. A. Alpers, working in the Historical Archives of
Goa at Panjim, Goa, discovered fourteen letters in Swahili, in
the Arabic script, with Portuguese translation. These were
dated, according to the translation, between 1711 and 1728.
Though some of these letters were written from Kilwa, an
initial comment by Mr M. H. Abdulaziz, of the Department of
Language and Linguistics, University College, Dar es Salaam,
suggests that the Swahili in which they were written is not too
dissimilar from his own Ki-Mvita. One awaits the more detailed
study of these letters with the greatest interest, but if it is
assumed that such letters were written – despite the translation
into Portuguese – with an expectation of being understood,
then one might have some evidence for a hypothesis that the
form of Swahili which served as a lingua franca among the
coastal towns as far south as Kilwa was a northern rather than
a southern variety of the language. Clearly we need to know
much more about the sender, the scribe, and their relation to
other elements of the local population, but the discovery is an

exciting one for the history of Swahili. Since neither the
Tambuka manuscript nor the letters can be regarded as representing an early stage in the development of the language,
we can now reasonably infer that a northern-type variety of
Swahili was being spoken on the coast at least as early as the
seventeenth century.

What, then, can be said about the earlier period? The present
evidence from comparative Bantu is not incompatible with
Bantu-speaking communities being on the coast well before the
tenth century A.D., but actual linguistic evidence from this
early period is both meagre and inconclusive. Distinctions are
made, however, throughout the early period between the pagan
tribes of the mainland and the Islamized coastal settlements.
The most important of these were on the offshore islands of
Faza (Pate), Mombasa, and Kilwa, at Malindi on the mainland,
and on the islands of Pemba, Zanzibar (Unguja), Mafia, and the
Comoro: their political fortunes have been described in some
detail by the historians, but of the language spoken by their
inhabitants prior to the eighteenth century, they can tell us
virtually nothing. As the language of Islam, Arabic must surely
have been pre-eminent, both for communication with the outside world and for communication up and down the coast;
indeed, one might guess it was the language of the *élite*. But
what other languages were spoken, what language was spoken
to the mainland Africans who came down to the coast to trade?
Of these we have no more than tantalizing fragments, tempta-
tions for the unwary, and tasty morsels for each new generation
of myth-makers. Yet there is one point that should be made
here; whatever the language of the 'port-towns', it did not
need to leave the coast much before the beginning of the nineteenth century. So long as trade with the interior could be
carried on by representatives of trading networks in the interior
coming down to the coast, rather than by initiating expeditions
from the coast, the incentives for communication were largely
of a low order and lay with the sellers. When the expansion of

D

trade shifted the initiative to caravans from the coast, the need for an effective lingua franca became acute, and Swahili came into its own.

FURTHER READING

HISTORICAL

There is an increasingly large selection of books and articles on East African history to which the interested reader may turn. On the one hand, there are general studies like *Zamani: a survey of East African History*, B. A. Ogot and J. A. Kieran (eds.) E.A.P.H. and Longmans, 1968; on the other hand, there are the specialist articles in the *Journal of African History*. The following titles may serve to stimulate further interest and most provide detailed bibliographies:

ERIC AXELSON, *Portuguese in South East Africa*, Witwatersrand, 1960

JOHN GRAY, *History of Zanzibar*, O.U.P., 1962.

G. S. P. FREEMAN-GRENVILLE, *The Medieval History of the Coast of Tanganyika*, O.U.P., 1962.

G.S.P.FREEMAN-GRENVILLE, *The East African Coast*, Clarendon, 1962.

R. OLIVER and G. MATHEW (eds), *The History of East Africa*, Vol I, Clarendon, 1963, esp. Chapters I–VI.

J. E. G. SUTTON, *The East African Coast*, Historical Association of Tanzania, Paper No. 1, E.A.P.H., 1966.

J. S. KIRKMAN, *Men and Monuments on the East African Coast*, Lutterworth, 1964.

LINGUISTIC

The first volume of Prof. M. Guthrie's four-volume *Comparative Bantu* appeared early in 1968. Until the later volumes are published readers are referred to the article listed in footnote 4, and to that following:

'Bantu Origins: A Tentative New Hypothesis', *Journal of African Languages*, Vol. I, 1, 1962.

There are two general surveys of the Bantu languages:

M. A. BRYAN (comp.), *The Bantu Languages of Africa*, O.U.P., 1959.

M. GUTHRIE, *The Classification of the Bantu Languages*, O.U.P., 1948.

Useful introductions to historical linguistics generally are:

J. GREENBERG, 'Historical Linguistics and Unwritten Languages', in *Anthropology To-day*, ed. Sol Tax, Chicago, 1962.

W. P. LEHMANN, *Historical Linguistics: an Introduction*, Holt Reinhart, 1963.

SWAHILI HISTORICAL TEXTS

The best known of these, the Kilwa Chronicle, is discussed in detail in Freeman-Grenville (1964) referred to above. A more general discussion of such texts is to be found in Prins, A. H. J., 'On Swahili Historiography', J.E.A.S.C., Vol. 28/2, 1958, 26–40.

III · The Diffusion Up-country

. . . The importance and value of the Swahili language with reference to future work can scarcely be over-estimated. It appears to be, indeed, the trade language of Eastern Africa, so that a person, possessing an acquaintance with it would be able to make himself understood even far away in the interior of the country.

U.M.C.A. Report for 1868, p. 11

The expansion of Swahili inland from the coast falls into two phases: in the first, from about 1800 to 1850, the country was gradually opened up by trading caravans, who took the language with them in the form of a Swahili-speaking 'managerial' core; during the second phase, from around 1850 until the advent of the Colonial Powers, the first systematic studies of the language were made and used as a basis for teaching others.

At the outset of the century Swahili was still essentially a language of the coast, serving, we may suppose, as a means of communication for the network of trading communities along the coast, from Mikindani in the south to Lamu and Pate in the north. At the northern end, on the islands of Faza and Lamu, it was, additionally, the medium for a sophisticated literature in the Arabic script, devoted to praise of the Prophet, and to the propagation of his teaching. About this time the verse tradition began to spread southwards to Mombasa, taking on a more secular role in the process, and serving as a medium for Mazrui resistance to the Busaidi of Zanzibar. Consider, for example, this poem of Muyaka bin Haji (1776–1840), who may justly claim to be Swahili's first nationalist poet:

MUGOGOTO WA ZAMANI

Mugogoto wa zamani   ule muukumbushawo
Na uoneke ngomani   ukihimu watezawo
Wake na makao nduni   nduni namba si ya yewo
Yunga na Kiwa-Ndewo   na Mkongowea weni

Jifungetoni masombo   mshike msu na ngawo
Zile ndizo zao sambo   zijile zatoka kwawo
Na tuwakalie kombo   tuwapigie hariwo
Wakija tuteze nawo   wayawiapo ngomani

Na waje kwa ungi wawo   tupate kuwapunguza
Waloata miji yawo   ili kuja kujisoza
Na hawano waiyewo   wana wa Mwana Aziza
Sijui watayaweza   au ni kuongeza duni

Wajile wajisumbuwa   hawa na wana wa Manga
Kutaka lisilokuwa   ni maana ya ujinga
Kulla siku twawauwa   na kuwakata kwa panga
Mwaka huno ukizinga   hawaji tena mwakani[1]

(The previous threat, which, you recall, became war, hustled up the men, the women, and those at home; you people of Pate, Lamu, and Mombasa fortress, I tell you it is not like that today. (ii) Tighten your loincloths, take up sword and shield, these are your vessels. They may have come from their parts; let us intercept them, and challenge them, if they come let us join with them, when they come out on to the field of battle. (iii) Let them come in hosts so that we may reduce them, they who left their homes to commit suicide, and they include the sons of Queen Aziz; whether they'll succeed or add to their misery I don't know. (iv) They have come bringing trouble on themselves, they and the Arab sons of Manga. To want what you can't have is idiocy. Each day we'll kill them and cut them down with our swords, when this year ends they'll not come next.)

Farther south still, a combination of factors was contributing to the development of a new situation in which a language was required not for communication along the sea routes but for communication along the inland trade routes. The initial development of these inland routes as a response to the increased demand for ivory was made possible by the existence of Zanzibar as a long-established trading centre for the coastal trade in ambergris, gum-copal, hides, etc. Writing in 1828, the American trader Edmund Roberts noted that:

> . . . there were at Zanzibar, exclusive of (military) transport, dhows, upwards to two hundred fifty sail of dhows, *bagalas* and other craft with pilgrims, drugs, fish, coffee, water etc. from Suez, Mocha, Jedda, the seaport of Mecca, and the island of Berbera in the Red Sea, the ports in the Persian Gulf, the coast of Africa as far south as Mozambique, and I saw but a small part of their commerce.[2]

Equally important was the gradual accumulation there of expertise and capital derived from custom dues. This latter fact had been noted in the previous century by the Frenchman Morice, who regarded it as one of the reasons in favour of setting up a base on the mainland, and his compatriot Guillain was like-minded:

> Bref, il a été clairement démontré que les articles d'importation ayant à Zanzibar une valeur moindre qu'à la côte d'Afrique, en même temps que ceux d'exportation n'y sont achetés qu'à un prix plus élevé, il y aurait un double avantage, pour les étrangers, à aller sur le continent traiter directement avec les indigènes. Ce serait le seul moyen de dégrever l'échange des charges que font peser sur lui le courtage souhhéli et la concentration préalable, à Zanzibar, des marchandises offertes et demandées de part et d'autre.[3]

One might ask, however, why there was an upsurge of trading in this early part of the century, and here a brief historical digression is necessary.

The independence of the American colonies in 1776 freed them from restrictions on trade in the Indian Ocean. From early on in the nineteenth century, therefore, we find American ships arriving in Zanzibar with the rough cotton cloth from Massachusetts, whose provenance was to be perpetuated in Swahili in the word for such cloth, *amerikani* or *merikani*. Burton noted, for example, that of 41 ships which visited Zanzibar between 1832 and 1834, 32 came from America, and 20 of these came from Salem in Massachusetts. By 1856 the number of ships visiting the island had risen to 89, and again those from America were the most numerous, though by now the Germans and French were close behind.[3a] A formal treaty between Seyyid Said and the United States was agreed to in 1833, and the first American consul arrived in 1837. The French had been in the area since the previous century, and Morice's interest in setting up a trading post at Kilwa has already been mentioned. The Napoleonic Wars brought a stop to French trading activities in the area, and on the cessation of hostilities she occupied herself first with Madagascar and then with the Comoro Islands. A formal treaty between Seyyid Said and the French was not drawn up until 1844, when the first French Consul took up residence. The first German trading vessel arrived in 1843, following which trade increased rapidly, to the point where representatives of German firms were posted to the island.

As far as the British were concerned, trade in the Indian Ocean up to the end of the eighteenth century had been almost a private monopoly of the East India Company, but this had suffered somewhat during the Napoleonic Wars from attacks by French raiders based mainly on the Seychelles and Mauritius. With the capture of these islands, and their cession to the British under the terms of the Congress of Vienna, Britain's attention was drawn to the existence of a slave trade in the area, and ships of the Royal Navy made their appearance along the coast with increasing frequency. A British Consul was established on Zanzibar in 1841, but at this period the British appeared to have been less interested in trade than in the suppression of the slave trade.

By the early 1840s, then, several countries had established formal trading relations with Zanzibar and the island's trading figures began to rise markedly.

Another important factor in the initial stimulus of trade was Seyyid Said's decision in 1828 to take personal charge of his East African domains. It was some time before he could deal with the rebellious Mazrui in Mombasa, but increasingly he was able to turn his attention to measures designed to increase his revenue. He encouraged the development of clove-plantations by his followers and kinsmen from Oman, and some forty-five plantations were ultimately established. He was also responsible for financing trading caravans, at least from 1839 onwards, though caravans had been opening up the trade routes for some years prior to that. An Arab colony was established at Ujiji on Lake Tanganyika by the early 1840s, and at Tabora some time before that. The first Arab caravan reached the Court of the Kabaka of Buganda, Suna, in 1843. The effect of such ventures as these on the revenue was gratifying: one estimate of the revenue in 1828 gives a minimum figure of $30,000 (c. £6,000), but by 1844 the annual rental paid by the farmer of the customs had risen to $125,000 and continued to rise. It is noteworthy that in 1870, when Tippu Tip set off on his third major trip, he was backed to the extent of $50,000 worth of trade goods.

There had, however, been a steady trickle of trading caravans before this date: Tippu Tip's own grandfather had acquired a reputation as a caravan leader, which had probably been made by the twenties. The governor of Zanzibar had financed an expedition to Unyamwezi around 1824 which brought back some twelve tons of ivory. A little later the American trader Edmund Roberts wrote to an American Senator that while in Zanzibar he had frequently seen elephant hunters return from 'thirty days' journey' into the interior, and his countryman, E. Burgess, *en route* for the Mission field in India, in 1839, learned that the Sultan sent expeditions up-country every cool-season which might be away a whole year. Yet to travel on these caravans was no picnic: even large caravans, Burton was told in 1857, were liable to many hazards. In his autobiography, Tippu Tip gives a vivid account of some of these; disease, famine, trouble with porters, and local hostility:

> ... On reaching URungu our rations were exhausted; there was famine there and no food! A serious situation! We had a large caravan too, of more than 4,000 men. ... We reached the borders of Itawa, ... Here there were many villages and a great deal of cassava. ... The local people soaked it in water for six or seven days. ... When we arrived, the Nyamwezi and our slaves started to chew the stuff raw, since they had been hungry for some time. ... By the next morning 700 men were overcome, vomiting and with diarrhoea. ... Forty of them died.[4]

Clearly, powerful incentives were needed to draw the caravans on, and it was the promise of large profits which encouraged wealthy Asians in Zanzibar to finance them, becoming yet more wealthy. Much later in the century the German Carl Velten collected some Swahili traditions relating to the financing of these caravans, and it is worth while quoting at length from them. I have translated very freely from the original:

> ... A Swahili wishing to make a trip, goes to talk to an Asian, his patron, and says to him, 'I've come to you Mukki. I want you to lend me some goods because I want to make a trip.' His patron will reply, 'I'm not refusing, but go and bring along some reputable person to come and act as your guarantor, then I'll give you the goods.' The man will reply, 'I haven't got a guarantor, I have only myself, just have faith, let me have your property willingly and without resentment, everything is the work of God, and by His

Will I shall return and you will have cause to be glad.' His patron will reply, 'Very well, I've heard what you have to say, but let me think about it.' They will part and the man will ask, 'When shall I come for your reply?' 'Come in a week's time.' When the week is up he'll go to his patron and tell him, 'I've come for your verdict.' He'll ask, 'How much capital have you? Have you a farm or house?' 'I've nothing, I tell you, trust in God, and if I'm alive, honest to God, I'll give you your due.' His patron will reply, 'All right, but I want you to sign an official receipt.' 'I'm quite willing to do that.' 'How much stuff do you want?' '£200's worth.' 'For how long?' 'Two years.' 'Too long, make it one!' He'll settle for one year.

When they've reached agreement they'll go to a Government official to sign the receipt for £200, and the official will affix his signature. They'll go to the shop. He'll ask, 'What kind of goods do you want?' 'I want 15 lengths of cotton cloth and 10 of coarse stuff – this is all ordinary white stuff. I also want some length for clothes.' 'What kind?' 'I want some dark red, and some with blue background, chequered in white with multi-coloured borders, also some "rehani", and some multi-coloured cloths, some with silken and gold threads, some blue cotton with embroidered edges, and some "heart-break"; plus a tub of beads, four sacks of shell-ornaments, seven boxes of sugar, six "kata" (a measure, rather more than 6 lb. each) of brass wire, and a tent.'

Having added these up, he'll also need the porters' fee, he'll agree with the porters the size of his loads, and each porter will get half his fee. When they've got their fee they must fasten up their loads. When they've done this, he'll go to his patron to say good-bye. 'Good-bye and good luck.' The traveller will set off.[5]

In none of these early accounts is there any direct evidence for the use of Swahili, but we do know that the trading caravans usually included a number of people from the coast who were certainly Swahili speakers. In Macqueen's account of Lief ben Saied's journey into the interior in the early thirties, Lief had about 500 people with him, including 'about seventy' of his own followers.[6] This again constitutes no more than evidence that Swahili would be spoken within the caravan, but in view of the linguistic diversity of the areas through which the caravans passed, it is reasonable to suppose that Swahili proved itself a most useful medium of communication, at least in the trading context. The point is explicitly confirmed by Burton:

> My principle being never to travel where the language is unknown to me, I was careful to study it (i.e. Swahili) at once on arriving at Zanzibar; and though sometimes in the interior question and answer had to pass through three and even four media, immense advantage has derived from the modicum of direct intercourse.[7]

Perhaps the best testimony for the increasing utility of the language comes from the increased sophistication of the material collected on it, all at the coast it is true, but then this was the starting-point of the caravans and the centre of the Swahili-speaking world. By the late 1840s European knowledge of Swahili was being systematically extended by the work being carried on in Mombasa by the C.M.S. missionary J. L. Krapf, which appeared as *Outline of the Elements of the Kisuaheli Language with Special Reference to the Kinika Dialect*, Tübingen, 1850, giving a new dimension to the words and phrases which had appeared up till then. Some of these, like the short notes of H. C. von Gabelentz and H. von Ewald (*Zeitschrift der Deutschen Morgenländischen Gesellschaft* I, 1846–7) were based on Krapf's work, but others were collected independently by explorers, sailors, or merchants, such as S. K. Masury, an early American resident of Zanzibar whose vocabulary was printed in 1845 in the *Memoirs of the American Academy*. His compatriot, J. L. Wilson, also had a vocabulary printed in the first volume of the *Journal of the American Oriental Society*. It was to be more than a hundred years before the Americans took up the systematic study of the language, when they, too, became involved in a type of Missionary work.

TABLE I
EARLY WORD LISTS

	Sowauli (Salt, c. 1811–13)[8]	Sowahili (Smee, c 1811–12)[9]	Sowheli (Ross Browne 1843)[10]	Souahhéli (Guillain/ Vignard 1846–8)[11]	Sidi (Burton, 1845–9)[12]
Nouns					
Fire	mo-to	moto		moto	moto
Iron		tchoomar	chu-ma	tchouma	komongo
Water	mo ye	mety		madji	májí
House	ne yum bá ne		youm-ba	nioum'ba	nyumbá
Mountain	ma-toom bé			m'lima	
God		mooangur	m'goo	mouézi monggo	
Fish		summakee	soo-ma-ke	en'çi, soumaki	sonbá
Rain		foo, ar		em'vona	vurá
Wind		paepo		p'hépo	
Sun		toow, ar		djoua	juwa
Cow		gnombai		m'gôm'bé	ngombe
Sheep		cundow		kon'doo	khundoro
Thief			m'-we-ve	moévi	
Smoke			mo-she	mouchi	
Cloud			ma-ving-oo	ouignegou	mawingo
Thunder			oo-ma-me	râadi	
Bow			oo-ta	mtchâré	pinde
Spear			m'coo-ke	m'kouki	mukok'í
Firewood			cooney	kouni	
Basket			ke-ka-poo		
Oil			ma-foo-ta	mafouta	
Fly			n'za	in'zi	
Teeth			ma-no	minou	menú (a tooth)
Hair				gnouéli	nyoere
Leg				mégoûou	muguru (foot)
Eye					máchho
Beard			da-voo	an'dévou	devo
Chest				kéfoua	
Son	ma-to to			m'toutou	mtoto (child)
Father	babbe-akoo			baba	babayá
Young girl	se ja na			kidjana	viyakází (daughter)
Numerals					
1	che-mo jé	mouya	moya	modja	moyà
2	mab-be-re	beetee	beeli (5 in text)	m'bili	perhí
3	ma-da too	patoo	tatoo (2 in text)	tatou	táhtú
4	mú-ché ché	hinna	n'nee (3 in text)	inné	mme
5	má noo	tanoo	tanoo (4 in text)	tanou	tháno
6		sitta		sitta	thandatú
7	fun já te (6 in text)	sebla		sebâa	mfúngat
8	mun ná ne	nanee		nanné	mnání
9	muk en deh (7 in text)	kenda		ken'da	mpyá
10	ko-me (9 in text)	kooma		koumi	kummí

	Sowauli	Sowahili	Sowheli	Souahhéli	Sidi
Verbs (*Salt does not give any*)					
Bring			litta (? Imper.)	kouléta	
Carry away				koutchoukoa	ak(a)chukolá
Come			n'jo (? Imper.)	koudja	akáje
Die		koofa		koukoufa	
Fight		peeganah			
Give		neepai		kounipa	akánepá
Hear		selkia			
Hit				koupiga	
Like			se-penda (I don't like it)	koupan'da	
Sell		kooza		kouza	akábijá
Spill			oo-se-ma-gee (Don't spill it)	koumouaïka	
Steal			oo-ma-que-ba (You stole it)	kouïba	
Take					akáfengá

In addition Ross Browne gives a number of phrases, like:

> *soo-a-za-koo sem-ma-ma*, I can't stand up
> *ma-ca-ma-ta-ya-he?* How did you catch that?
> *be-o-rum ta-coo-o-na sha*, I'll show you
> *hoo-na-ne-here*, You will not say so

while Guillain/Vignard give not only six pages of phrases but a short grammatical sketch of the language as well.

Students of Swahili will note with interest that both Ross-Browne and Guillain/Vignard appear to have heard two different sounds in contexts where modern Standard Swahili would have 'i'. Ross-Browne distinguished 'e' and 'ee', while the Frenchmen used 'i' and 'é'. It is intriguing to speculate on whether the variety of the language which these observers listened to had seven rather than five significant vowels.

These vocabularies reflect the lack of any linguistic training or sophistication; the orthography is usually unexplained, and no indication is given of the place of collection nor of the informants used. Yet it is interesting to see the state of our knowledge at this time, not least because these fragmentary word-lists represent all our direct historical knowledge of the language. For this reason, in Table I I have set out a selection from five of the pre-1850 sources (excluding the Payton vocabulary from Chapter II). It is virtually complete in the case of Salt and Smee, but no more than a sample from the other three. The dates in brackets refer to the probable time of collection rather than the date of publication, which in one case was considerably delayed. Salt and Smee's material probably relates to dialects around or to the north of Mombasa, while Ross Browne's was collected in Zanzibar. The Guillain/Vignard material may have been collected anywhere, but from internal evidence it looks most like that of Zanzibar town. Burton's material was collected from slaves in Sindh during his tour of duty in 1845–9, and is not claimed to be Swahili. On the other hand, many of the slaves seem to have come from the coastal areas, and the 'sidi' language appears to have been one they could all speak. They mention 'Lamo, Baramaji (?Mboamaji, south of Dar es Salaam) and Kinkwhere (perhaps the language of the ŋhwele people, i.e. kiŋhwele, north of Dar es Salaam)'. Though they include members of some inland tribes, such as Nyamwezi and Sagara, many are easily recognizable as coastal groups, e.g. 'Dengereko, Makonde, Matumbi, Gindo, Mudoe, Mzigra, etc.' Mr R. B. Patel, of Nairobi, tells me that there is still a Swahili-speaking 'Sidi' community in Kathiawar: in the remote Gir forest some 200 miles S.W. of Ahmedabad.

As the century passed the half-way point, Missionaries added their number to the Arab caravans and European explorers who increasingly criss-crossed East Africa. During this period Swahili penetrated south-westwards into what is now Zambia and westwards into what would become the Congo republic. There are still residual communities in Zambia and along the Congo river, as well as the much larger settlements in Ujiji, Bujumbura (Usumbura), and Tabora. Yet it is important for the subsequent history of the language to note that it was predominantly in what is now Tanzania that the most effective expansion of the language took place. The main trade routes went from points along the coast, like Bagamoyo, Saadani, Mboamaji, and Kilwa through Ugogo to Tabora, or south-westwards, skirting Uhehe, to the gap between Lake Nyasa and Tanganyika. From Tabora caravans went west to the Lake at Ujiji, north-west to Karagwe and Uganda, or north to Lake Victoria, near the modern Mwanza. On the other hand, there was little expansion at this period from the Mombasa area towards Nairobi, because of the threat from Masai raiders, and the route into Uganda went round the west of Lake Victoria from Tabora.

The C.M.S. had maintained a Mission at Mombasa since the forties. Here Krapf and his colleagues, working on Swahili and the neighbouring languages, produced not merely the first grammar but the monumental dictionary. The major expansion of mission activity, however, occurred in the twenty years between 1860 and 1880. The U.M.C.A. established a Mission on Zanzibar in 1864; at Magila, in the foothills of the Usambaras not far from Tanga, in 1875; at Masasi, in the south in 1876, and, three hundred miles west, on Lake Nyasa, in 1881. The French Holy Ghost Fathers arrived in Zanzibar in 1863, and set up a mission on the mainland opposite at Bagamoyo in 1868. The C.M.S. started at Mpwapwa in 1876, the London Missionary Society at Ujiji in 1877, and the White Fathers at Tabora in 1878. Most of these centres were points along the trade-routes, so that the newly arrived missionaries had some lines of communication; nevertheless, the early mission stations led a precarious existence; Masasi, for example, was sacked and burned by raiding Ngoni only six years after its foundation. By far the most important centre for the study and propagation of Swahili was the Universities Mission centre at Zanzibar, where the redoubtable Edward Steere produced in 1870 the first edition of the *Handbook of the Swahili Language*, which was to remain in successive editions the standard grammar for students until well into the twentieth century. Awareness of differences between the Zanzibar dialect and that of Mombasa, described by Krapf, certainly contributed to the speedy compilation of this entirely new study – despite the somewhat acid comments of Krapf in the Preface to his dictionary – and these differences were to be emphasized rather than otherwise in the succeeding years. The importance to Missionaries of the time of Swahili is well stated by this gifted linguist in the Preface to the first edition of the *Handbook*, and in reading this one should not forget that he had already found time, in the six years since his arrival, for studies of Nyamwezi, Shambala, and Yao:

> There is probably no African language so widely known as the Swahili. It is understood along the coasts of Madagascar and Arabia, it is spoken by the Seedees in India, and is the trade language of a very large part of Central or Inter-tropical Africa. Zanzibar traders penetrate sometimes even to the western side of the continent, and they are in the constant habit of traversing more than half of it with their supplies of Indian and European goods. Throughout this immense district any one really familiar with the Swahili language will generally be able to find someone who can understand him, and serve as an interpreter.
>
> This consideration makes it a point of the greatest importance to our Central African Mission that Swahili should be thoroughly examined and well learnt. For if the members of the Mission can go forth from Zanzibar, or, still better, can leave England already well acquainted with the language, and provided with books and translations adapted to their wants, they will carry with them a key that can unlock the secrets of an immense variety of strange dialects, whose very names are as yet unknown to us. For they will not only be able at once to communicate with new tribes but in mastering this really simple and far from difficult language they will have learnt how to set about learning and writing all others of the same class, since they agree with Swahili in all the chief respects in which it differs from our European tongues.[13]

As Steere himself had found, none of these early Missionaries could afford to neglect the study of the local languages, but so numerous and diverse were they that if some basic areas of communication could be covered by Swahili this did much to facilitate initial contacts. The C.M.S. Missionaries at Mpwapwa, for example, discovered that once they had mastered their first few words of Swahili 'they could be sure of finding interpreters and an attentive audience'.[14] As the Missions penetrated into areas away from the trade-routes they found that Swahili was not always so useful, while other Missions avoided the use of a lingua franca on principle as being unfitted to reach the innermost thoughts of those undergoing the conversion to Christianity. This was particularly true of the German Moravians in the Southern Highlands of Tanganyika and the Lutherans in the Usambaras, to the west of Tanga. This view has been widely held, particularly in Kenya and Uganda, but it is worth noting that the two great pioneers of Swahili studies, Krapf and Steere, had no such doubts. Steere, in the previously quoted preface, describes it as '. . . a language which, through its Arabic relations, has a hold on revealed religion, and even on European thought while, through its Negro structure, it is exactly fitted to serve as an interpreter of that religion and those thoughts to men who have not yet even heard of their existence'. A more typical view of the relationship between Swahili and the local languages was that expressed by the U.M.C.A. Missionary, H. W. Woodward, 'A large number of men, however, can talk Swahili fairly well. Still, for many years to come, it will be necessary for missionaries to learn Boondei, if they would understand and be understood by the people generally.' Such views nothwithstanding, published material grew steadily, especially from the U.M.C.A. in Zanzibar: not merely studies of the language but readers and religious material. The first French grammar appeared in 1879, but the great German effort was reserved for the period of their administration of the area which was soon to follow. Consideration of this fact prompts one to suggest that there are, perhaps, two main reasons why one should learn the language of another man; in order to trade with him, or to have power over him, religious or political. This chapter has considered the first and to some extent the second: it remains to consider the political reasons for language study.

E

FURTHER READING

As a general introduction to this period of history, the most useful source is *History of East Africa*, Vol. I, eds. R. Oliver and G. Mathew, Clarendon, 1963, especially Chapter V onwards. The works of Sir John Gray cited in footnote 2 should also be consulted.

Of the various travellers who crossed East Africa I find Burton good company, though infuriating! Of his works the most relevant are:

The Lake Regions of Central Africa, 2 vols., London, 1860; new ed. 2 vols., London, 1961.
Zanzibar, City, Island and Coast, 2 vols., London, 1872.

Reference might also be made to the *Last Journals* (ed. H. Waller) of David Livingstone, 2 vols., London, 1874.

Fascinating reading – the adjective is not too strong – is provided by Alan Moorehead's *The White Nile*, Hamish Hamilton, 1960, though only Part I is really relevant to the time and place being discussed here.

For an account of trading caravans one cannot do better than consult Tippu Tip himself, *Maisha ya Hamed bin Muhammed, yaani Tippu Tip* (trs. W. H. Whiteley), recently reprinted by the East African Literature Bureau, Nairobi, 1966.

One should also consult:

R. W. BEACHEY, 'The East African Ivory Trade in the 19th Century', *J. of African History*, Vol. VIII, 2, 1967, 269–90.

N. R. BENNETT, 'The Arab Impact' being Chap. 11 of *Zamani: a survey of East African History*, B. A. Ogot and J. A. Kieran (eds.), E.A.P.H. and Longmans, 1968.

H. BRODE, *Tippu Tip*, Berlin, 1905.

ANDREW ROBERTS, 'The History of Abdullah ibu Suliman', *African Social Research*, Vol. 4, 1967, 241–70.

T. WAKEFIELD, 'Routes of Native Caravans from the Coast to the Interior of Eastern Africa', *JRGS*, Vol. 40, 1870.

IV · The Colonial Period

We are so many boys in this house (St. Andrew's College, Kiungani), and of different tribes, Yaos, Makuas, Bondeis and Nyassas; but we all speak Swahili language.

Yohana Abdalla to Isabel Hall,
2 January 1894, USPG Archives (London), UMCA A/5[1]

From the turn of the century, and increasingly with time, the educational and administrative implications of Colonial policies determined the choice to speak or not to speak Swahili. Though educational policies in Uganda, Kenya, and Tanganyika converged for a time in the 1920s, in general quite different policies were pursued in relation to Swahili, both in the British-administered areas and in the Belgian Congo, and quite separate treatment must be accorded them.

German East Africa/Tanganyika (including Zanzibar under British administration)

In the year 1885 Bismarck granted a charter to the Society for German Colonization, to develop those territories it had acquired as a result of the efforts of Carl Peters and his fellow adventurers. Thus it was that Tanganyika, as it was later called, came under German jurisdiction, though it was not until after the 'Bushiri rebellion' of 1888–9 had been crushed that Germany accepted administrative responsibility for the new colony.

One version of the Bushiri rebellion is preserved for us in a Swahili poem, composed less than five years after the event. In some ways it is a puzzling poem, for it is not clear for whom it was composed, nor for what purpose. In common with other such poems of the period it is retrospective and documentary: gone are the stirring phrases with which Muyaka sought to stiffen Mazrui resistance against the invaders from Zanzibar. The poet tells of the arrival of the Germans on the Mrima coast and of the negotiations with the Sultan of Zanzibar for 'control of the shipping', i.e. the ports:

> The letters came to every single place and the chiefs and governors received the news. We waited for a whole month and in the second month we heard news. We were assured that Europeans were living in the houses of the town of Pangani. It was said there were two. The name of one was Nyundo (lit.: hammer. This was Haupt. E. von Zelewski who was killed on a punitive expedition against the Hehe in 1891, when his force was virtually annihilated). The second was Kitambara (lit.: cloth. H. von Wissmann (?) who was Governor in 1895–6). He had crossed to the further bank and had built at Bweni. Two days later we heard that two Europeans had arrived and settled on the mainland. We heard that they had reached Bagamoyo. They wanted all the towns; indeed they had bought them. At Kilwa and Dar es Salaam there was a plague of Europeans. There was no free speech; they held the country. To Tanga they came daily asking for houses, and some who had obtained them were already established. At Winde and Sadani the towns were full of Europeans and into all the harbours ships came daily. In all the harbours wherever you looked you could see war-ships, every day, I tell you.[2]

Similar poems sought to document, often from the German point of view, the punitive expeditions against the Hehe, under Mkwawa, the campaigns around Kondoa, and against Hasan bin Omari, between 1893 and 1897, but again there is no evidence at all as to the audience for whom they were composed. They were collected by the German scholar, C. Velten, published with a German translation, and have remained in libraries ever since.[3]

In the areas where traditional local authorities complied with German requirements the framework of a local administration developed slowly; junior officials, usually from the coast, having limited powers over groups of villages. Such a system was undeniably inefficient, but unavoidable, bearing in mind the high coast of using German administrators, yet the attempt to administer such a vast area with minimal resources led to the misuse of the delegated powers by *akida* and *jumbe*, and to popular uprisings of the Maji-Maji type, again documented for us in a Swahili poem. Here the poet complains specifically:

If you want the reasons for this uprising, we shall not withhold them but reveal them openly. Bwana wetu (there is no adequate translation for this phrase which combines here both respect and servility), we are tired of being under orders. We would rather die and have done with it. This is our choice. We have to cultivate our fields, pick cotton in the evenings, then build our houses and look for our tax-money. A heavy burden as we saw it. All night we talked things over, we plotted revolt, and have chosen to die.[4]

But the Germans were not unaware of the problems: a school was established in Tanga in 1893[5] to train Africans to occupy places as junior officials, and by 1903 there were eight government schools, twelve local authority schools, and fifteen mission schools.[6] As Swahili was to be the language of the administration, great efforts were made to document it, and scholars like Velten, Seidel, Büttner, and others provided the materials on which Courses at the Oriental Seminar in Berlin were based. A governor like Rechenberg (1906–12) spoke the language, and his successor, H. Schnee, had attended Courses in Berlin. Competence, however, was not a monopoly of the administration; settlers and missionaries, too, became competent in spoken Swahili, even though missionaries in general concentrated their attention on local languages. Education expanded steadily: by 1911 the Missions were responsible for the Primary Education of 30,000 pupils, the Administration for that of 3,500, while 2,500 pupils were receiving industrial or higher education.[7] A school population requires textbooks, and these were produced in increasing numbers: here the British missionaries of the U.M.C.A. had led the way since 1870, and in 1905 the Mission at Magila produced the 'classic' *Habari za Wakilindi*, an account of the early history of the Shambala. The first part of this remained, for fifty years, a legend of stylistic excellence, until a copy found its way to the East African Swahili Committee in the fifties and republication was made possible. The U.M.C.A. were also responsible for the first newspapers, *Msimulizi* (1888) and *Habari za Mwezi* (1894?), and these were followed in 1910 by the German Protestant Mission's monthly *Pwani na Bara*, whose circulation had risen to 2,000 by 1914.[8] The first issue, of four pages, contained an article on the Kaiser's birthday; notes on the Nyamwezi chief Mirambo; on the area of the coast known to the local Zaramo as Mzizima, later to be renamed Dar es Salaam; statistics on the number of lion and leopard killed; comets; and the development of Zeppelins. The Catholics followed with *Rafiki Yangu* in the same year, a monthly with a much more pronounced religious leaning. In 1910, too, the series of religious booklets, *Barazani*, sold 11,000 copies, evidence for the existence of some kind of reading public.

By 1914 the Administration was able to conduct much of its correspondence with village headmen in Swahili; indeed, letters not written to the Administration in either Swahili or German were liable to be ignored.[9] This was one feature of German Administration which proved of great value to their successors, the British, and evoked a good deal of approval in later years. The Report on the Territory for 1921, for example, stated '. . . the late German system has made it possible to communicate in writing with every Akida and village headman, and in turn to receive from him reports written in Swahili'.[10] Such advantages could be shared by administrators and administered alike. For the former it was convenient to have a single language in which high standards could be imposed on officers and maintained throughout their service. For the Education Department it meant that problems of staffing were minimized and those of textbooks simplified, particularly once some form of standardization had been achieved.[11] It also meant that the Junior Service, staffed by Tanganyikans, was not restricted to regional postings; and members could be transferred without difficulty from one part of the country to another and be sure of finding a small community of Swahili speakers round the 'boma'. There is also some evidence that it engendered a sense of belonging to a unit larger than the tribe,[12] though the situation varied considerably across the country, according to various factors, such as the scale of administration, the size of the District headquarters, the extent of counteracting tendencies among local Missions, and the attitudes of local groups to their own languages. In some areas, for example, Sukuma, Mbulu, Ha, Nyakyusa, Swahili was not used widely until much later.

Over the whole Colonial period Swahili was used throughout the District Administration as a means of communication between people and officialdom, not only where this was the only possible means of communication but also, in some cases, where English could have been used. It was thus a mark, if only secondarily, of social distance; a means of reaching down to people, rather than of enabling them to reach up to the administration. Whereas in German times the acquisition of Swahili represented a first stage towards participating in Government through membership of the junior Civil Service, no further stage in this participation could be achieved through the language. The next stage involved the acquisition of English, and for this reason Swahili was seen increasingly by Tanganyikans as a 'second-class' language. It was used as the medium of primary-school education and as a subject up to the Cambridge School Certificate, but the medium of instruction in Secondary Schools and of Higher Education was English. As time went on the difference in the quality and quantity of secondary-school materials and teachers was clear evidence to pupils, if to no one else, of the inferior status of the language. Institutions of higher education in East Africa designed primarily for East Africans made no provision for the study of Swahili, while their use of English simply confirmed East Africans in their belief that it was on this language that they should set their sights. While the language of the lower courts was Swahili, the language of the higher courts was English. While Swahili newspapers were plentiful, the glossy magazines were in English. If Tanganyikans went to the cinema they saw English, American, or Asian films.

When TANU was founded in 1954 it was well placed to reap the benefits of a long-established and consistent language policy. Its success justified and reinforced that policy at a time of considerable criticism from educationists.[13] It is easy, in retrospect, to criticize the scale, the organization, and some-times the direction of the policy at this period, but by the mid-fifties it was certainly being more widely and more vigorously applied than hitherto. There were, for example, as many as forty newspapers in regular circulation. A majority of these were run by the Government: well-intended, uncritical hand-outs of Government policy, for the most part unimaginatively presented. Others were produced by the Missions, and one or two, like *Zuhra* in Dar es Salaam, were independently run. Among the Government papers one must distinguish between the 'regional' and the 'national' Press. The regional papers, more than twenty, usually appeared monthly, and were concerned almost exclusively with local, i.e. district, news. Consider the following examples:

Kulichi. Sumbawanga, monthly, four pages, for December 1953: Editor's notes; girls' education in the district;

letters from readers; district news, including a report on a recent Council meeting; items from the Courts; care of local graves, etc.

Mara Gazeti. Tarime, monthly, four pages, for December 1952: Detailed account of a stormy meeting between the D.C. Musoma and the people of Uzanaki. Rest of issue given over to advertisements.

Irgobawe. Mbulu, monthly, six pages, for June 1958: Planting of coffee; extract from Census; note of annual TANU meeting in Arusha; farewell to local D.C.; readers' letters; discussion on health; advertisements; football report.

The national papers like the famous *Mambo Leo*, which had been appearing monthly since 1923, and *Mwangaza*, which by 1957 was already a daily, dealt with Tanganyika news and any world news which merited attention. Consider *Mwangaza* for a typical issue during June 1957:

Page 1: important local or world news; page 2: Tanganyika news, e.g. lion killed with spear; page 3: readers' letters; page 4: more news from Tanganyika, football.

Yet these newspapers performed a valuable service; not only did they serve to establish Swahili as a means of national communication but they also introduced Tanganyikans to the problems involved in running such papers and provided adults with much-needed reading material.

Swahili records, also, were plentiful and very popular, though the form of the language in which they were cast was very far from the 'Standard' form approved for use in schools. The following is a sample from a typical song of the late 1940s, sung by 'Frank (Humplinck) and sisters' in the style of the American Andrews Sisters:

I greet my girl friend, 'How do you do?'
She's startled and swings round
She asks why I'm calling her an *mdudu* [insect].

I'm amazed, stupefied
I explain to her it's an English greeting
That's how one greets one's friends when one meets them.

[The Sisters chime in with

Listen, my good friend, I don't want any jokes, eh, eh,
Don't annoy me, my friend, I don't want to be called an
mdudu
Even you're an *mdudu*, even you're an *mdudu*.]

There are many fools like this one
Claiming they don't know English
When they're drunk, they just rattle it off
'How, *mdudu*, how do you do?'
Listen how they speak English
It's not 'broken' nor is it the real thing.

[The Sisters chime in with some broken English, including the
line

Give me *sigara*, hullo, freni mai.]

An interesting example of forms much more commonly found
in Nairobi than in Dar es Salaam. (Recorded on Gallotone GB
2251.)

Government Departments, too, notably Agriculture, were at
this time producing a considerable volume of Swahili material,
and work had been started on legal translation and on the
compilation of technical word-lists, essential preliminaries if
Swahili was to assume the status of a modern African language.[14] Furthermore, the technical advances which made
possible the production of cheap radios gave the Tanganyika
Broadcasting Services a vastly wider audience for its Swahili
programmes. Finally, the important step was taken in 1955 of
introducing simultaneous English/Swahili interpretation at
the sittings of Legislative Council, members being also permit-
ted to speak in Swahili where the Speaker was satisfied that
they would otherwise be hampered.

The value of Swahili to TANU was quickly demonstrated, and President Nyerere once boasted that during his many tours of the country he had had recourse to interpreters only on two occasions.[15] Not merely were the Swahili-speaking communities round the 'boma' fertile sources of recruitment but they also served as an excellent example when the Party wished to organize its own country-wide branches. It might be true that President Nyerere's status as a leader was enhanced by his ability to negotiate for independence in English, on terms of linguistic equality, but in this role the fact that he represented so large a proportion of the people of Tanganyika was due in large measure to the efficacy of Swahili as a means of communication on a national scale.

Kenya

There is a certain irony in the fact that while it is Kenya that can boast of her eighteenth- and nineteenth-century Swahili literature, it is in Tanzania where most has been done for the development of a Swahili literature in this century. Though Kenya has a long coastline, along which Swahili is spoken as a first language, this coastal form has never been accepted up-country; while the various up-country varieties of Swahili that have developed (especially among Nilotes, Asians, European settlers, and residents of Nairobi) have never been adopted on the coast. The European settler variety of Swahili (Ki-Settla) in particular, with its limited vocabulary, highly attenuated grammatical structure, and occurrence in invidious social contexts did a great deal to encourage the myth that Swahili was unfit to cope with the requirements of the twentieth century, and discouraged any consistent policy.

As early as 1906, Sir Charles Eliot made a strong plea for the learning of the local language to increase administrative efficiency,

... To my mind the greatest desideratum for improving our native administration and establishing friendly relations with the tribes which are still remote and diffident, is a wider knowledge of native languages. As a rule, officers only know Swahili – the 'lingua franca' of the Protectorate, which is more or less understood by many natives of the interior, just as many Europeans understand French. But the more important chiefs cannot, as a rule, speak any language but their own ...[17]

Shortly after this speech the problem of whether English or Swahili should be the lingua franca of the Colony was voiced for the first time at a United Missionary Conference held at Nairobi in 1909, in connection with plans for primary education. It was to be raised at frequent intervals in the years that followed, and visiting Commissions gave the protagonists on both sides ample opportunities of stating their case. Government made a number of pronouncements on policy, of which that of the Education Department for 1929 seems to be representative, thus 'It is the policy of the Government to establish English as the "lingua franca" of the Colony as soon as possible' (p. 17) and 'The vernacular will be used for the first four years of school life' (p. 18). The value of the local language was also stressed by Kenyan officials giving evidence before the Select Committee on Closer Union in East Africa.[18]

In practice, Swahili was widely used by officials and unofficials alike to suit administrative convenience, but its relegation in many contexts to the status of a basic means of communication won it few adherents, and reactions were not slow in coming. In education it was used both as a medium of instruction and taught as a subject, but nowhere was it surrounded with an aura of prestige comparable to that of English. The Missions continued their practice of using local languages, and by 1936 could point with pride at the number of gospels that had been translated, but in many ways they were out of touch with local aspirations. Government officers, for their part, were always in favour of learning a local language,[19] but extenuating circumstances could always be adduced as a reason why this had not been done. Just how effective these circumstances proved was not brought out clearly until the outbreak of the Emergency in the fifties, when the shortage of competent Kikuyu speakers was dramatically revealed. At the same time, however, during the 1950s, Swahili was taken as a subject in the Kenya African Preliminary Examination after eight years education, by several thousand children, and considerable numbers took it at School Certificate level, though one suspects that it was taken as a soft option rather than from a conviction that it merited study along with other school subjects. There was also a quite remarkable proliferation of Swahili newspapers during these years, even more than in Tanganyika, but whereas a majority of the Tanganyika papers were produced in the regions, as many as three-quarters of the Kenya papers were published in Nairobi, and were altogether more ambitious in their presentation and content. The weekly *Tazama* had a circulation of nearly 17,000 in 1954, and one of the incentives for reading it seems to have been its fiction content, which included the serialization of a Peter Cheyney type novel and a translation of *Blanket Boy's Moon*. Swahili 'pop' records, too, were more plentiful than in Dar es Salaam, and singers from the Congo proved very popular,[20] though 'purists' from the coast preferred the more traditional Swahili songs with their Arabic and Asian musical influence. In short, if Swahili was the language of the country in Tanganyika, in Kenya it was the language of the towns, especially Nairobi, where people from all parts of the country found it a convenient bulwark against the loneliness of city life as well as a ready tool to exploit the attractions which the city offered. Even so, the varieties of Swahili in current use raised many problems: the variety used by the Kenya Broadcasting Corporation in its up-country programmes was unacceptable to coastal speakers, just as the coastal forms found no sympathy up-country; the more conservative people up-country preferred their own language, anyway, to a form of Swahili which they knew from varieties heard on programmes from Tanganyika to be 'inferior'.

With the approach of independence, the two political parties adopted vigorous but by no means consistent language policies, which seem to me to be typical of the ambivalent attitude that has characterized all language policy in Kenya. KANU, committed politically to centralism, started off by advocating Swahili as the language for the whole country and produced their party newspaper in it; later, however, perhaps in deference to their party membership, they favoured the three main local languages, Kikuyu, Kamba, and Luo. By contrast, KADU, committed politically to regionalism, increasingly favoured the use of Swahili, again reflecting the bulk of their members' affiliation to the smaller tribal units. On the other hand, Swahili was, of course, of crucial importance to both parties, whatever their avowed policy; though the threat from English as the language of the progressive, go-ahead young citizen was growing rapidly. Writing on Kenya's first General Election in February 1961, George Bennett and Carl Rosberg commented with reference to the English language qualification for candidates:

> The vernacular could be used to appeal to fellow tribesmen, but if a wider African audience was to be reached, Swahili was essential. Indeed a candidate could not follow the election in the open seats without being able to read the national Swahili press. The English requirement eliminated the old Swahili-speaking leaders, and helped to point up the fact that a young, new generation of educated men was coming to power.[21]

Uganda

Here, particularly in Buganda, the Church has enjoyed an enviable esteem. C.M.S. Missionaries arrived at Mutesa's court, on his invitation, in 1876, the year following Stanley's visit, and White Fathers followed after an interval of only a few weeks. From the beginning it was clear that the Kingdom of Buganda was to occupy a central place in the affairs of the Protectorate, a matter which from the Ganda point of view was entirely right and proper, since, to quote from a letter submitted to the Committee on Closer Union by the Lukiko:

> It is a well known and admitted fact that the fundamental traditions and customs of the Baganda upon which the constitution of their kingdom is based are totally different from those of any other native tribe in East Africa.

From the first the Missions concentrated on Luganda, and it is a reflection of their industry that when Pilkington of the C.M.S. was killed in 1897(8) he had already prepared a grammar of the language and had translated the Bible. While such studies were, perhaps, a usual feature of C.M.S. activity, there seems to be no doubt that as time passed, such knowledge bestowed a gratifying sense of power *vis-à-vis* the newly arrived Protectorate officials, and may well have been a contributory factor to their unwillingness to see Luganda supplanted in any way. The appointment of Ganda Administrative agents to various parts of the Protectorate contributed further to the spread of the language, but here, the agents were often seen – as indeed they may have seen themselves – as extending the power and influence of Buganda, and in due course reaction against both language and people set in.

The position of Swahili, in this land of Christians, was jeopardized from the outset by its association with Islam, a rival and 'inferior' religion, about whose alleged vices apprehensive Christians of many denominations were prepared to unite. Whatever merits the language might have from an administrative point of view, and these were frequently voiced between 1910 and 1920, it is clear that for the Church it was an alien tongue and for the Baganda a thinly veiled threat to their status. In 1927 the Governor, Sir W. F. Gowers, wrote a Memorandum entitled 'The Development of Ki-Swahili as an Educational and Administrative Language in the Uganda Protectorate'. In it he proposed, among other things, that Swahili should be adopted as the lingua franca throughout a considerable part of the Protectorate – but *not* Buganda – for purposes of education. The parts concerned included portions of Eastern Province, excluding Busoga, and portions of Northern Province and West Nile District. It was not intended that the teaching of Luganda in Buganda should in any way be discouraged, though it was suggested that Swahili might be introduced as an extra subject in Buganda, as well as in Bunyoro, Toro, and Ankole. There seems to have been some opposition to these views, and the *Uganda News* of 22 February 1929 carried a Memorandum by the Kabaka, Sir Daudi Chwa, in which he made a strong protest,

> I feel, however, that it is my duty to add here in conclusion, that it is quite unnecessary to adopt the Ki-Swahili language as the Official Native Language in Buganda, and I am entirely opposed to any arrangements which would in any way facilitate the ultimate adoption of this language as the Official Native Language of the Baganda in place of, or at the expense of, their own language.

As the Kabaka subsequently admitted in a letter to his Saza Chiefs, the Protectorate Government had had no intention of taking such a step, and his original fears had been the result of a misunderstanding by himself. However, the Kabaka was not alone in his objections: the Bishops of Uganda also protested in a written Memorandum to the Secretary of State, in which they outlined the disadvantages of Swahili and put forward a number of reasons why Luganda should be preferred as a lingua franca. At about the same time, giving evidence before the Joint Select Committee on Closer Union in East Africa, Mr S. Kulubya made the following comment. Being questioned about his belief that Swahili was being introduced in Uganda, he replied, 'I should say that in most cases it is being forced, instead of being introduced.' But he admitted, 'It has not been forced so much in Buganda, but of course we never know what will happen.' In reply to a further question as to which second language he thought preferable, he was in no doubt at all, "English, of course, my Lord, which is the key to everything.'[22] From that date there was no further question of Swahili participating in Uganda's linguistic planning, though its use was continued in the police into the fifties, a fact which was commented on tartly by the Royal Commission.[23] There was, however, some justification for its continued use in the northern parts of the country, where constables were likely to be in contact with people unfamiliar either with English or Luganda. It is interesting to note the support for Swahili among the Nilotes in Uganda, in contrast to the opposition from them in Kenya, which does something to dispel the myth that there are linguistic reasons why Nilotes find Swahili difficult to learn, In Uganda, where the Nilotes were weak in relation to the Lake Kingdoms, notably the Ganda, Swahili was both a unifying influence and a means of buttressing their position by stressing the links with Swahili speakers elsewhere. In Kenya, where the Luo were a relatively powerful group, Swahili served to diminish their position by merging them with the rest of the Bantu-speaking groups of the country. Swahili did not disappear from Uganda, however, but persisted and flourished on the football field and in various other situations where use of English or Luganda was neither desirable nor possible. As a subject for debate in the Legislative Council, it reappeared during the 1960 discussion of the annual £800 subvention to the East African Swahili Committee,[24] a subvention which seemed

F

annually in jeopardy, but which had been maintained since the thirties. Members argued eloquently, if irrelevantly, for or against it as a national language, and a similar view informed a resolution of the Uganda People's Congress in the same year,[25] but no official reaction resulted.

The Belgian Congo (including Ruanda-Urundi)

Three main factors contributed to the emergence of Swahili as one of the Congo's four major 'trade' languages. Tippu Tip, more than any other single person, was probably responsible for the introduction of the language into the eastern Congo during his trading expeditions from 1870 to 1884. When these Swahili traders opposed the setting up of the Congo Free State and were defeated by the Belgians many of them settled in the area, constituting little Swahili-speaking islands of Bangwana or 'freemen', their language being known as Kingwana, though, as we shall see below, the term also covered other varieties. A second factor was the recruitment by King Leopold II of soldiers from Zanzibar, and until around 1914 Swahili was used for the training of soldiers in Katanga and the Oriental provinces. The third factor was the development of the mining industry in Katanga, whose demands for labour were met by the introduction of workers from the north-east, who used a variety of Swahili as a trade language. Subsequently there emerged in Katanga an urban population who used a form of Swahili as a mother tongue. In these eastern and south-eastern parts of the country Swahili was used by the local Missions in the lower forms of the primary school and as a means of communication by the local administration, but its further expansion was blocked by the emergence of other important means of communication, each with its own protagonists among Missionaries and Administrators. Foremost of these were Lingala, increasingly the language of the Force Publique and of the Army; Luba, in Katanga; Kongo, around Leopoldville, and

Mongo, in the areas to the south-west of Stanleyville. Each of the last three was spoken by a large number of people.

Yet the linguistic diversity of this country, wherein almost 200 languages were spoken, not by any means all Bantu, impressed on the Belgians the need for some national African language. While it was clear that French would become such a national language for educated Congolese, it was also evident that these would represent only a very small *élite*, one of whose tasks would be to 'créer une littérature indigène'.[26] But which of these 'indigenous' languages should be chosen, and if one of the four major languages *were* selected (Swahili, Lingala, Luba, Kongo), which variety should be chosen? The Swahili spoken in Katanga differed markedly from that of Stanleyville or that around the shores of Lake Tanganyika. Among the objections raised to Swahili as such a national language during the thirties and forties was that it was not a Congolese language, that it encouraged the propagation of Islam, and that it was already the official language in British East Africa:

> Mais ce qui doit nous determiner à écarter le Kiswahili même sous le nom de Kingwana comme langue officielle du Congo Belge, c'est qu'il est déjà la langue officielle de toute l'Afrique orientale anglaise. Il va soi que son évolution ultérieure nous échapperait entièrement.[27]

The question, unsolved during the thirties, was raised again at a meeting of the Institut Royal Colonial Belge in 1944. The need was again stressed for a national language to establish links both between tribes and between European and African, as well as to serve as a country-wide medium for the dissemination of culture and education. Such a language must not be a language 'd'importation européenne' but rather 'une langue véritable', neither a lingua franca nor a *sabir*.[28] On this occasion the case for Swahili was argued clearly and forcibly: it was a language that had been widely used in the country for many years; it had a considerable literature and had already been

standardized; and its use in the Congo would immediately
create a large Swahili-speaking block from the east to the west
coast, as well as opening up the possibilities of links with the
British-administered areas of East Africa.[29]

In the event, none of these languages was selected, each
continued to operate within its own sphere until independence.
So far as Swahili was concerned, it remained the most important
means of communication within the south-eastern and eastern
parts of the country; there was a certain amount of secular and
religious reading material, several newspapers, and a certain
number of language courses.

On the other hand, no serious attempt seems to have been
made to achieve a unification of all its various dialects, though
in the eastern part of the country efforts were made to achieve
some standardization of Kingwana. But what was meant by
Kingwana? In an illuminating article on the language situation
in the Congo, Polomé, talking of the Swahili communities left
behind in Maniema after the departure of Tip pu Tip, comments,
'The dialect spoken by those communities is known as ki-
Ngwana.'[30] A few years earlier Harries, from experience in the
eastern part of the Congo, had written:

> The statement has often been made that the Swahili traders
> in the Congo spoke the dialect of Swahili known as King-
> wana, but this term applies more rightly to the lingua franca
> *as spoken by the Congo peoples*. The distinction should clearly
> be made, for even today in the Swahili settlements the people
> of Swahili origin speak a form of the language much more
> closely related to standard East African Swahili than do the
> tribal Africans who use the language only as a trade lan-
> guage.[31]

A Belgian writer gives an even wider definition:

> Ce qu'on parle souvent comme *lingua franca* au Congo Belge
> (provinces D'Elisabethville, de Costermansville et de Stanley-

ville), ce n'est pas le *kiswahili*, mais le *kingwana*, langue
simplifiée, dérivée du kiswahili.[32]

Whatever is being covered up by the use of such a label, it is
clear from other evidence that considerable differences are
involved, both between the varieties of Kingwana and between
Kingwana and standard Swahili. All the varieties of spoken
'Kingwana' seem to share a highly simplified grammatical
structure, with a phonology and lexicon devoid of Arabic
sounds and words respectively. The Katanga varieties have
been influenced by their Bantu Luba-speaking milieu, while the
north-eastern varieties have been affected by non-Bantu-
speaking peoples. Harries gives a short description of one
variety from which the following examples are taken.[33] Standard East African Swahili versions are appended in brackets:

kitabu ile nilinunua (*kitabu nilichonunua*), the book I bought
mie iko na watoto tatu (*mimi nina watoto watatu*), I have three
children
mie hapana kula hata mie moya (*mimi sili hata peke yangu*, I
don't even eat by myself
kama unakatala kusadiki, paka utakwenda ku fasi ile (*kama
ukikataa kusadiki lazima uende mahali pale*), if you refuse
to believe you must go to that place. Note the use of the
Arabic – sadiki.

In the Eastern Congo efforts seem to have centred on con-
forming to East African standard Swahili or on the creation of
some kind of standard Kingwana. In the earlier period the
Catholics favoured the former, the Protestants the latter, but
subsequent to 1945 there were increasing efforts to introduce
something approaching standard East African Swahili, either
through the schools or through a written medium like the
Press. The work of the Swedish Missions both here and in
Ruanda-Urundi may be taken as an example of this, though it
may be that they attempted too close a conformity with East

African usage for the milieu in which they were working, cut off as they were from regular supplies of East African Swahili materials. The efforts of the Protestants at Nyankunde in the north-east, cited by Harries, are also noteworthy for their attempt to produce a standard form of Kingwana. Here a newspaper, *Neno la Amani*, was produced and a new translation of the Bible undertaken. As Harries observes:

> The result is basic Swahili plus many Kingwana idioms and minus any true Swahili style, but even so it is a step towards standard Swahili and is not envisaged by the missionaries as a permanent form of Swahili. It is exclusively literary, for no one, not even the missionaries, speaks this basic Swahili, but it is bound to affect the speech of those who come to know it, familiarising them with basic Swahili grammar.[34]

As is pointed out here, such attempts to propagate a standard form of the language result in a marked divergence between the written and spoken language which is neither quickly nor easily reduced. Yet this need not be a source of dismay, for there is little in the field of language planning which can be achieved rapidly. Provided the model is disseminated thoroughly and consistently over a long period, there is no reason why assimilation should not take place in the long run, provided, of course, that there is no deep-seated hostility to the language. The production of detailed courses such as E. Natalis's *La Langue swahilie*, Liège, 1960, is certainly a valuable beginning. However, policies such as these were all placed in jeopardy at the assumption of independence, since the premise of language policy itself underwent change.

Marginal areas – a footnote

The most important of the marginal areas are the Comoro Islands, in which varieties of Swahili, e.g. Ngazija and Nzwani, have been spoken for many years. At the present time the position is that French is the official language, but notices aimed at the general public are issued in French and Ngazija, usually in the Arabic script. Kiunguja is spoken by a large minority, but has no official status.[35]

At the other end of the Swahili-speaking area, off the Horn of Africa, lies the island of Socotra, where a variety of Swahili, probably a northern dialect, seems to be spoken by a large minority of the population.[36]

Farther south on the Somalia coast, at Brava, is spoken the variety known as Ci-Miini, and there are probably other pockets of Swahili speakers between Brava and the Kenya border. Some Swahili is also spoken in Malawi and northern Madagascar.

FURTHER READING

The most useful general source for this period is the *History of East Africa*, Vol. II, eds. Vincent Harlow, E. M. Chilver, Clarendon, 1965.

Many of the references in the footnotes constitute valuable additional reading, but some more specialized titles may be noted.

TANGANYIKA

T. O. BEIDELMAN, 'A History of Ukaguru: 1857–1916', *Tanganika Notes*, 58–9, 1962, 10–39. Contains a useful bibliography.

R. F. EBERLIE, 'The German Achievement in East Africa', *Tanganyika Notes*, 54, 1960, 181–214.

G. C. K. GWASSA and JOHN ILIFFE (eds.), *Records of the MAJI MAJI Rising*, Historical Association of Tanzania, Paper, No. 4, E.A.P.H., 1967.

J. P. MOFFETT, *Handbook of Tanganyika*, Govt. Printer, Dar es Salaam, 1958. A good factual account of Tanganyika during the Colonial period.

O. F. RAUM, '(II) German East Africa: changes in African life under German Administration, 1892–1914', *History of East Africa*, Vol. II, Vincent Harlow and E. M. Chilver (eds.), Clarendon, 1965.

KATHLEEN M. STAHL, *History of the Chagga People of Kiliman-jaro*, Mouton, 1964.

MARCIA WRIGHT, 'Swahili Language Policy 1890–1940', *Swahili*, Vol. 35/1, 1965, 40–9.

KENYA

GEORGE BENNETT, *Kenya: a Political History*, O.U.P., 1963. A good, short account.

N. S. CAREY JONES, *The Anatomy of Uhuru*, Manchester Univ. Press, 1966

BELGIAN CONGO

D. BIEBUYCK and M. DOUGLAS, *Congo: Tribes and Parties*, R.A.I., 1961. Useful very brief summary.

L. W. HAMISS KITUMBOY, 'Kiswahili Usages, Congo Belge and Ruanda Urundi' *Swahili*, Vol. 31, 1960, 227–30.

L. W. HAMIS KITUMBOY, 'Swahili in Ruanda Urundi and Congo Republic', *Swahili*, Vol. 32, 1961, 65–6.

MARIA LEBLANC, 'Evolution linguistique et relations humaines', *Zaire*, Vol. 9, 8, 1955, 787–99. A detailed examination of language loyalty in Katanga.

B. LECOSTE, 'A Grammatical Study of Two Recordings of Belgian Congo Swahili', *Swahili*, Vol. 31, 1960, 219–26.

ZANZIBAR

JOHN MIDDLETON and JANE CAMPBELL, *Zanzibar: its Society and its Politics*, O.U.P., 1965.

V · 'Standard' Swahili

The chaps who speak Swahili here
Have never heard of Bishop Steere
Sometimes a really zealous learner
Some concords may pick up from Werner
But 'safi' stuff is heard alone
When Ratcliffe talks to Elphinstone.

G. A. R. Savage[1]

Though each of the three East African countries pursued different language policies, there was sufficient agreement among all three for a small subvention to be voted annually to an organization known originally as the Inter-Territorial Language (Swahili) Committee, later known simply as the East African Swahili Committee. Though the Committee did not come into existence until 1 January 1930, its existence was presaged by an Education Conference of 1925, convened by the Governor of Tanganyika and held in Dar es Salaam. The objective of the Conference was the selection of a language which would serve as a lingua franca for use in as large a number of schools as possible right across the Territory, educational theory at that time holding that for local education 'it is an incalculable advantage that a common vernacular language should be as widely used as possible'.[2] Swahili was selected as the most suitable language by virtue of its predominance over large areas of eastern and 'equatorial' Africa. At the same time it was recognized that there were dialectal and orthographic variations in the language, and that if it were to be used throughout the educational system a common orthography and dialectal form for the written language were essential, whatever variations in spoken language occurred. As long ago as 1882 Krapf had foreseen the problem:

> What confusion must arise, if the University Mission at Zanzibar, the Church Missionary Society's agents at Frere Town and in Uganda, the Free Methodists at Ribe, the Scotch Mission near Lake Nyasa and the London Society near Lake Tanganyika, would have their separate orthography![3]

In 1926 a number of proposals were formulated relating to the spelling and word-division of Swahili, together with a list of new and forthcoming books which generally conformed to these proposals. During the year an experiment was tried in the monthly paper *Mambo Leo* of using 'c' instead of the previously used 'ch', but this proved unacceptable and was dropped. At various times, too, suggestions were made that the velar 'n', as in the English si*nging* and Swahili *ng'ombe*, cow, should be spelled with an 'ŋ', rather than the clumsy 'ng'', but they were all rejected by Education Departments. These proposals, which were later adopted as the basis for 'Standard' written Swahili, were criticized in points of detail over the years, but as a result of their adoption and implementation in the preparation and publication of school textbooks a standard written form of the language was largely achieved during the thirties and forties.

As an immediate result of the 1925 Conference, a Central Publishing Committee was set up. This body was to be kept informed of the details for all projected secular school text-books, so as to avoid all unnecessary duplication of effort.

The problems of standardization for education rapidly became acute: the Kenya Government's Language Board had tried in 1927 to set some kind of standard for Kenya, and Tanganyika soon proposed further co-operation. In June 1928 an inter-territorial Conference was held in Mombasa, attended by the distinguished linguist Prof. Meinhof, at which the decision was confirmed to adopt the dialect of Zanzibar, sponsored by the Universities Mission to Central Africa, in preference to that of Mombasa, advocated by the Church Missionary Society. Differences between scholars from these two areas were of long standing, and the bitterness which this decision engendered was slow to subside: during the thirties and forties the Mombasa dialect was associated with separatism and conservatism. This was doubly unfortunate: the richness of the historical and literary traditions of Mombasa and the northern coast, together with their links with Islam, seemed to offer little of relevance to the rest of Kenya, which tended to look towards the Swahili of Tanganyika; but the south lacked any such traditions, and their absence from school syllabuses in both Tanganyika and Kenya certainly impoverished the Swahili Courses of several generations of students. Against this, however, the adoption of a variety closely akin to varieties of the language already spoken over large areas of inland Tanganyika contributed powerfully to its rapid acceptance.

After the Conference the Acting Colonial Secretary of Kenya circulated a letter to the other Governments on the question of setting up some body which would supervise the standardization so far agreed upon:

1. There would appear to be no question but that it is desirable to have complete inter-territorial co-operation both in the preparation of any new dictionary and grammar and in the constitution of a committee for selection, revision and translation of educational texts.
2. That it is considered that a full time secretary should be appointed whose salary would be provided by contributions from the various territories, this secretary to be stationed at such a place as should be mutually agreed upon by the territories concerned.

In January 1929, as a result of further recommendations by the Education Advisory Committee, Tanganyika, the question of the urgent need for the establishment of such a body was communicated by the Secretary of the Conference of East

African Governors to the four Governments, and on their approval a draft scheme was circulated and agreed upon with the Secretary of State's approval. A letter was conveyed from the Under Secretary of State for the Colonies to the Secretary of the Conference of East African Governors, and the Inter-Territorial Language Committee came into being on 1 January 1930.

Initially the Committee consisted of seventeen members, the Director of Education and one official, and two non-officials from each country, Kenya, Uganda, Tanganyika, and Zanzibar, together with the Organizing Secretary. African membership of the Committee dates from 1939, when one member from each country was appointed, but no full meetings were held during the war years, and it was not until 1946 that Africans participated in the meetings. At the outset the Committee was based in Dar es Salaam, but moved to Nairobi in 1942; in 1952 it moved to Makerere, but it moved back to the coast ten years later, to Mombasa, before finally returning to Dar es Salaam in 1963. There, in 1964, it was finally incorporated into the Institute of Swahili Research, one of the Research Institutes of the University College, Dar es Salaam. In those thirty-four years it can at least be claimed that standardization was achieved, but more than that, foundations were laid for the development of Swahili as a modern African language. Mistakes were certainly made, more could undoubtedly have been done, but with the resources available the achievements remain an impressive tribute to the many men and women who gave unstintingly of their energies.

The central aim of the newly founded Committee was 'to promote the standardization and development of the Swahili language', and to this end the Constitution set out a number of ways by which this could be achieved:

(i) Standardizing orthography and obtaining complete inter-territorial agreement.

(ii) Securing as far as possible uniformity in the use of existing and new words by the exercise of control over the publication of school and other dictionaries.

(iii) Securing uniformity of grammar and syntax throughout the publication of standard books on the subject.

(iv) Giving encouragement and assistance to authors whose native tongue is Swahili.

(v) Giving advice to all prospective authors concerning books which they propose to write.

(vi) Procuring the revision where necessary of the language of approved Swahili textbooks and books of a general nature already published.

(vii) Drawing up an annual programme of Swahili books required under the headings (a) Textbooks, and (b) General Literature

(viii) Making arrangements for translating into Swahili of the textbooks and books of a general nature selected, or for direct authorship in Swahili of such books.

(ix) Examining and where necessary correcting the Swahili of such textbooks and general literature before publication.

(x) Revising and giving advice concerning the matter of all Swahili books that are dealt with by the Committee.

(xi) Supplying authors with information as to methods of teaching in vogue in the various territories.

(xii) Answering general inquiries regarding Swahili language and literature.

(xiii) Undertaking such other activities as may be deemed incidental and conducive to the attainment of the foregoing objects.

It will be convenient to divide the operations of the Committee into four periods: first, the eighteen years between 1930 and 1947 under the aegis of the Conference of East African Governors; the period under the jurisdiction of the East Africa High

Commission, 1948–52; thirdly, the 'Makerere College' period, which lasted from 1952 to 1962; and the final period, which covers the return to the coast, under the administration of the University College, Dar es Salaam.

The main emphasis during the first period was on standardization, and the most important achievement during this period was undoubtedly the revision of Madan's *Swahili–English Dictionary*, a project which started as a revision, but which ultimately developed into the preparation of a new dictionary by the Committee's first Secretary, Frederick Johnson. Work was started in 1933, and though Johnson did not live to see the work in print, his successor, B. J. Ratcliffe, guided it through the press, and it appeared in 1939. No dictionary can even aim at perfection, since language is constantly changing, but on its appearance it was readily acknowledged to represent a great step forward in Swahili lexicography. A new dictionary is now being prepared in the Office of the successor to the Committee, the Institute of Swahili Research, thus continuing the tradition so ably established by Johnson.

With reference to the task of standardizing projected textbooks, the procedure was as follows. All suggestions regarding new books and manuscripts came to the Committee from the Directors of Education, to whom copies of the work in question were sent for consideration. The Secretary of the Committee was then informed, as soon as possible, whether the book in question was approved for use in schools, how many copies would be required initially, and how many annually. The Secretary then saw to their translation, after making arrangements with publishers, or arranged for the publication of an entirely new work on the subject required. Those books that were written or translated into Swahili, together with those that were sent in to the Committee for revision of the language, were forwarded to two of the Committee's Readers for perusal, comment, and suggestion, thus ensuring the uniform standard orthography as decided on by the Committee as a whole. The

Imprimatur of the Committee was granted when the Secretary was satisfied that the recommendations approved by the Committee had been incorporated in the author's text.

Reactions to the end product of this process were not slow in coming. In the Committee's *Bulletin* for 1934 there appeared a Memorandum by a member of the Kenya Education Department, raising a number of points which were to be discussed on many occasions during the next twenty years. Commenting on the process of standardization, he says:

We have standardised Swahili and in the process Swahili seems to have become a new language. While, doubtless, all are ready to admit that Swahili, like any other language is bound to develop and grow, in form, idiom and vocabulary, as a result of the impact of the civilisations of the immigrant communities, yet surely the development must come from the Swahili mind, and must not be superimposed on them from without. But that is just what we have tried, and are still trying to do, with the result that we are in the somewhat ludicrous position of teaching Swahilis their own language through the medium of books, many of which are not Swahili in form or content, and whose language has but little resemblance to the spoken tongue. We are perhaps too apt to overlook the fact that the people themselves are not only capable of adapting their language to modern needs, but are doing so with amazing rapidity.[4]

In the same issue there appeared a second Memorandum, which in part answers some of these points, but which also deals with a number of general issues. While agreeing that the development of Swahili must primarily be the work of Africans themselves, Broomfield maintained that there were, nevertheless, three areas in which the continuing influence of Europeans was desirable in the situation as it obtained at the time:

(i) The composition of dictionaries and grammars, where

European scholars had a range of knowledge and experience not then accessible to Africans.

(ii) The adoption of new words, where consultation and co-operation between the Europeans, as introducers of new concepts, and the African, as repository of knowledge about Swahili, was essential.

> That is the way we work, and by means of the I.L.C. there are several people in each of the territories making enquiries about the same words. Then the Committee meets and we compare our results. Different suggestions are put forward, and the Committee decides which are the most satisfactory. A list of words recommended by the Committee is then published. Ideally, it might be better to make no suggestions at all, and just wait for Africans to evolve new words when they felt the need for them, but life is not long enough.[5]

(iii) The selection and cultivation of standard forms of grammar, syntax, etc., from material written in many different dialectal forms:

> I have also had MSS from different parts of Tanganyika, and some of them have had peculiarities of their own. What is one to do? It is quite obvious that the time has not come when all our books can be produced in one identical form of the language. One has to bring them into agreement so far as is possible without creating too much ill-feeling. The European, with his training in linguistics, is the person best fitted to attempt this, and it will help towards a gradual assimilation of one dialect with another. Kiunguja must be the basis, but, as it seems to me, all the main dialects will contribute something to the future. Further, Swahili is developing everywhere and, if left to itself, will develop in different ways in different localities.[6]

Now it is clear that the process of selection is a delicate one, in which the right balance between over-standardization and freedom of expression is extremely difficult to achieve. It may be that in the early days when there was an acute shortage of trained Africans too heavy a burden was placed on the Europeans, whose intuitive control of the language was inadequate for the task in hand. Something of this appears in a further criticism from the writer of the first Memorandum:

> There is one other general point which must be noticed. Most of the Swahili contained in these books is correct grammatically, and may be defended on that ground. Grammatical accuracy, however, does not of itself constitute a language, and it is perhaps this very exaggerated application of grammatical rules that has led us away from the real Swahili language, and made us substitute something which is at its best lifeless, though intelligible, at its worst both lifeless and unintelligible.[7]

In the early days of standardization such criticisms, however merited they were at the time, were probably less justified than they were subsequently, when an over-rigid application of the standard forms did appear to give books written in Standard Swahili an artificial and stilted style, evoking from many Africans the label 'kizungu' or 'kiserikali' (European or Governmental). Yet one must recognize with Broomfield that the process of standardization and unification is an extremely difficult one: many of those who sought to implement the recommendations were imbued with a sense of urgency to get books written, to get them into the schools, and to get as many Africans educated as possible in the shortest possible time. Many of those who worked for the Committee were dedicated and humble men, deeply conscious of the enormity of the task before them. Some of those who appeared to manipulate the language so arrogantly knew that if they stopped to consider alternatives they would make no decision at all.

G

On 1 January 1948 the East African High Commission came into being, taking over the functions of the East African Governors to which the Committee had been attached since its inception, and for the next four years the Committee passed under its jurisdiction. A new Committee was formed, comprising two representatives from each of the four Governments, and the Secretary, B. J. Ratcliffe, who had taken over the onerous task on Johnson's death in 1937, retired at the end of 1949. Until the appointment of a new Secretary in 1952 the activities of the Committee were directed by C. G. Richards, Director of the East African Literature Bureau, and H. E. Lambert, Swahili's most distinguished scholar until his death in 1967.

This was a period of change, both in the outlook of the Committee and in the climate of opinion within which it worked. Any pre-war agreement on educational policies in the various countries had long since given way to divergence, and the place of Swahili in those policies was yielding, to a greater or lesser degree, to English. The major drive to get Swahili books into the schools had slackened, the new standard dictionary had been published, and a new organization, the East African Literature Bureau, had been set up to deal with all publishing matters. While the pattern of change for many Government Departments was expansion, that of the Committee remained static, its annual budget of around £2,000 in 1930 rising to £2,200 in 1951. In short, the Committee left the stage and moved into a back room! The change in role has been well summarized by the Committee's Chairman at the time, R. A. Snoxall:

But it may be objected that the Committee has diminished its number, does this represent progress? I think it does. The solution of the earlier administrative difficulties, and the production of school textbooks, then the primary needs, have meant that the work of the Committee has developed from the earlier stage of administration, regulations and legislation, to the stimulation of authorship, the introduction of words, and the consideration of truly linguistic problems by those most qualified and interested to do it.[8]

While the Literature Bureau took over the literary role of the Committee of stimulating authors, initiating competitions, etc., it was agreed that the Committee should remain the authority on matters of Swahili research and orthography, and these changes were reflected in the revised constitution.[9] Increasingly, however, there was mention of research, and at the annual meeting of 1950 the view was expressed that:

> Research work in the Swahili language was stated to be of very great importance, and it was observed that there is at present no other Organization to undertake it. Research into indigenous Swahili literature was also recommended. Research into the present state of the Swahili dialects was considered to be a matter of importance.[10]

And among the activities proposed we find the following among a long list of suggestions:

(a) The presentation of adequate material for the study of Swahili.

(b) The constant revision of dictionaries and textbooks in the light of the results of research.

(c) Informing the East African public through the Press about the status, value, progress, and development of Swahili.

(d) Research into Swahili history, language, dialects; conservation and interpretation of indigenous and traditional literature.

(e) Maintaining contacts between the Swahili-speaking countries, Tanganyika, Zanzibar, Kenya, Uganda, Northern Rhodesia, Nyasaland, Somaliland, the Belgian Congo, the Comoro Islands.

The possibility of attaching the Committee to Makerere College arose during 1951, when it became known that the East African Institute of Social Research intended to start work on the linguistic side in 1952. The change was effected as from 1 September 1952, when the Committee became attached to the Institute. In that month I collected the Committee's crated effects from the Office in Thika Road, Nairobi, and removed them to the first of the series of offices that were put at the Committee's disposal during the next ten years. As a Research Fellow of the Institute I was able to devote only half my time to the Secretaryship of the Committee, and an evaluation of the Committee's activities seemed an important first step to working out a new programme. In the Annual Report for 1952–3 I summarized these as follows:

(a) The scrutiny and correction of manuscripts, with a view to their obtaining the imprimatur of the Committee for the conformity of the Swahili in which they were written, to the standard forms approved by the Committee. The scrutiny and correction of these manuscripts, between six and eight of which were received per month, occupied the greater part of Mr Lambert's time, in his capacity as Acting Secretary, during 1951.

(b) The issuing of a *Bulletin* compiled and edited by the Secretary, intended as a forum for the discussion of linguistic matters. This was printed free by the apprentices of the Government Printer, Dar es Salaam, appeared roughly every year,[11] and had a circulation of 500 to 600 copies.[12]

With reference to (a) it had been clear for some time that manuscripts were being sent in increasing numbers to the East African Literature Bureau, who were in no way obliged to send them to the Committee, and subsequently published without any marked diminution of standards. There was some variation from the standard forms, but this seemed in no way regrettable in literary works. It was decided, therefore, that the time had come to renounce, with the exception of school textbooks, the work of scrutinizing manuscripts for the imprimatur. With regard to (b) it was felt that an attempt should be made to bring the *Bulletin* out at specific dates, even if it meant putting the whole thing on a commercial basis and charging a subscription. So far as research was concerned, it was decided to concentrate on two projects: a study of Swahili dialects and a survey of current Swahili as evidenced by the Swahili Press.

During the next six years small-scale investigations of the dialects of Mombasa, Tongoni (Mtang'ata), Pemba, and Rural Zanzibar (Hadimu and Tumbatu) were carried out, particular attention being paid to the difference from Standard Swahili and to the extent to which the dialects were or were not being eroded by the use of a standard form. The results of this research, together with those of studies made earlier by H. E. Lambert on Vumba, Jomvu, Ngare, and Chifundi, were written up and published in a special series of Dialect Studies or in the Committee's *Journal*. Work proceeded more slowly on the survey of current Swahili, but the Committee's Research Assistant, O. B. Kopoka, produced a series of pioneer studies in Swahili grammar, in Swahili, which were only terminated by his resignation in 1958 to join the Shell Co. Reference should also be made to the series of historical supplements to the *Journal* which were initiated in 1955 and which were aimed at making available to the reading public some of the facts of East African history which had been originally written in Swahili, such as the Bushiri rebellion, the Maji-Maji rising, and Tippu Tip's own account of his trading ventures in Tanganyika and the Congo, which did so much to spread the language across the eastern part of the Congo. An additional task which was undertaken in 1955 was the compilation of a supplement to the standard dictionary, but though a great deal of useful work was put in, it was never possible to harness adequate resources to make this anything like as complete or as scholarly as was hoped for, even though preliminary versions were published in the *Journal*.

At this point something should be said of the Committee's *Bulletin* (renamed *Journal* in 1953 and *Swahili* in 1959). It is difficult to assess the value of such a publication in terms of its efficacy as a means of disseminating information on new words, standard forms, points of grammar, etc. Nor is it easy to estimate the extent of its impact: in the pre-war days, when it was distributed free, its circulation was largely restricted to Europeans, and it tended to be used as a kind of 'house' journal for the relatively small band of scholars actively engaged on the study and teaching of the language. Though 500–600 copies were distributed, large numbers went to Departments of Education and other Government Departments for an onward distribution which did not always take place. When I looked into this in 1952 I estimated that less than half of the total sent out from the Committee were actually circulated and read. In the fifties and sixties, when it appeared regularly twice a year, and there was an annual subscription, its appeal outside East Africa appeared much greater than within it, and appeals to readers to contribute comments to the various word-lists and dictionary supplements elicited a very poor response. In my quinquennial report for 1952–7 I said that, 'There is no doubt in my own mind that this is once again a function of the low esteem in which Swahili is held by Africans generally, which is in turn a reflection, in part, of the attitudes taken by Governments towards the language.'[13] I am not sure, on reflection, about the truth of this: it may have been unrealistic to expect a vigorous response to this kind of appeal. A distinguished Israeli linguist once told me that the modernization of a lexicon requires the leadership of a group of fanatics, to impose their views by the force of their chauvinism and convictions. Perhaps the climate of opinion was unfavourable when these carefully prepared and discussed lists of words were circulated: lists on all manner of subjects, from psychology and health via birds and fishes to electrical, nautical, and religious terminology. From the cyclo-styled lists of 1930 in *Bulletin No. 1* to the current work on the new dictionary which appeared in 1967 in Vol. 37/1 runs a skein of belief that the creation of a modern technical vocabulary should be a joint enterprise, a belief stemming from European diffidence in legislating for a language other than one's own. Yet, is the belief justified? Other countries have had to face this problem, what are the lessons to be learned from Turkey in the thirties and forties, from Malaya and China today, or from George Orwell's *1984*? We shall return to this problem in the final chapter.

On my return to England in 1959 J. W. T. Allen took over the Committee, and after a period of acute financial uncertainty was successful in negotiating a grant of £9,000 from the Calouste Gulbenkian Foundation, which was matched by a similar sum from Colonial Development and Welfare Funds. This provided for a Senior Research Fellow to be appointed, who would also take over Secretaryship of the Committee. On his arrival in 1961, J. Knappert supervised the removal to Mombasa and then to Dar as Salaam, where in 1964 the Committee was finally transformed into the Institute of Swahili Research within the University College.

If I say little about these final years it is not because they were not fruitful, quite the contrary. It is simply that during this period the focus of the Committee shifted increasingly away from education and standardization, away even from linguistic research, towards literary and historical studies and towards the collection and contextualization of new words. It may be, however, that, with the greatly increased use of Swahili in Tanzania during the past few years, coupled with the increasing production of books, some new effort in the field of standardi-zation may be required. This must surely be carried out by local scholars. One of the criticisms that can be levelled at the earlier period of standardization is that it was very largely carried out by expatriates. However great the justification for

this may have been, it did not contribute to local enthusiasm
for the language. Compare the position with that of English,
which was once itself a despised vernacular, with neither the
graces of French nor the authority of Latin; but the enthusiasm
of the sixteenth- and seventeenth-century English poets for
their language did much to validate the claims they made for it.
The following example from the *Musophilus* of Samuel Daniel,
a contemporary of Spenser and Shakespeare, is no isolated
paean of praise, but typical of many such that appeared in
prose and verse during the sixteenth century:

> Or should we carelesse come behind the rest
> In powre of words, that go before in worth
> When as our accents equall to the best
> Is able greater wonders to bring forth:
> When all that ever hotter spirits exprest
> Comes bettered by the patience of the North?
>
> And who in time knowes whither we may vent
> The treasure of our tongue, to what strange shores
> This gain of our best glorie shall be sent
> T'inrich unknowing Nations with our stores
> What worlds in th'yet unformed Occident
> May come refin'd with th'accents that are ours?[14]

Swahili was standardized from the outside, as it were, and only
Shaaban Robert shows anything like the vein of enthusiasm for
his language that runs through the English poets, who invested
their language with eloquence before orthographic or grammatical standardization took place. In Swahili the reverse
occurred, the standardization being effected on a non-literary
dialect during a period of Colonial administration. Inauspicious
augury for a national language. Independence is now redressing
the balance, and Swahili now claims some of the enthusiasm
previously reserved for English. East Africans will surely sym-
pathize with the sentiments of Roger Mulcaster, writing at the

end of the sixteenth century, when he exclaims, 'I honour the Latin but I worship the *English*', and he continues:

> But why not all in *English*, a tung of it self both depe in conceit, and frank in deliverie? I do not think that anie language, be it whatsoever, is better able to utter all arguments, either with more pith, or greater planesse, than our *English* tung is, if the *English* utterer be as skilfull in the matter, which he is to utter: as the foren utterer is. . . . It is our accident which restrains our tung, and not the tung it self, which will strain with the strongest, and stretch to the furthest, for either government if we were conquerers, or for cunning, if we were treasurers, not anie whit behind either the subtile Greke for couching close, or the statelie *Latin* for spreding fair. Our tung is capable, if our peple wold be painfull.[15]

FURTHER READING

To obtain an adequate idea of the extent and detail of the work carried on by the Committee to achieve standardization, reference should be made to the early *Bulletins* of the Committee, some of which are still available from the Institute of Swahili Research, P.O. Box 9184, Dar es Salaam, Tanzania.

The following more general works contain much that is relevant to the East African situation:

JACK BERRY, 'The Making of Alphabets', *Proceedings of the VIII International Congress of Linguists*, Oslo, 1958, 152–70.

P. GARVIN, 'The Standard Language Problem – Concepts and Methods', *Anthropological Linguistics*, Vol. 1, 1959, 28–31.

E. HAUGEN, *Language Conflict and Language Planning*, Harvard, 1966. Dealing with Norway's problems during the past hundred years.

U. HEYD, *Language Reform in Modern Turkey*, Oriental Notes and Studies No. 5, Jerusalem, 1954.

RICHARD FOSTER JONES, *The Triumph of the English Language*,

Stanford University Press, 1953. This detailed survey of opinions concerning the vernacular between 1476 and 1660 should be compulsory reading for all students of language planning. See especially Chapters 3 and 4 for loan-words and Chapter 5 for orthography.

P. S. RAY, *Language Standardization: studies in prescriptive linguistics*, Mouton, 1963

With particular reference to the East African situation, the following should be consulted:

G. W. BROOMFIELD, 'The Development of the Swahili Language', *Africa*, Vol. III, 1930, 516–22.

G. W. BROOMFIELD, 'The Re-Bantuization of the Swahili Language', *Africa*, Vol. IV, 1931, 77–85.

K. E. ROEHL, 'The Linguistic Situation in East Africa', *Africa*, Vol. III, 1930, 191–202.

J. WHITEHEAD, 'The Possibility of a Standardized Swahili', *Congo Mission News*, Vol. 55, 1926, 24–6.

J. and L. F. WHITEHEAD, 'Standard Kiswahili', *Congo Mission News*, Vol. 55, 1926, 22–3.

VI · After Independence

While we may expect that English will remain the language of our inter-national relations, and for a considerable time to come the language of higher instruction, there can be no doubt that Swahili is the more im-portant language. It has proved our greatest asset in our pre-independence struggle as the instrument of uniting the people of the nation's different tribes.

Leading article in *The Nationalist*, Dar es Salaam, 1 August 1966.

Each of the countries of eastern Africa brought to independence a bundle of attitudes and policies relating to language which they inherited from the Colonial period. Some of these attitudes, like that towards English or French, were bound up with the equation of the metropolitan language with 'being educated', or with the need to combat tribalism in a context where the use of a language like Swahili was simply not possible at that time, or with the short-term objective of achieving independence, an operation requiring expertise in the language of the Colonial Power.[1] In the years since independence a number of factors have contributed to the need both for retaining English or French and for developing whichever of these metropolitan languages had previously been neglected. The speed with which the University Colleges in Kampala, Nairobi, and Dar es Salaam have introduced French as a degree subject is altogether striking. Each of these countries belongs to larger political, social, and economic groupings, within which a metropolitan language is an essential medium of communication. Again, in the post-primary education of all these new states the metro-politan language is both the medium of instruction and the language in which all textbooks are printed. For such countries,

97

on whose slender resources so many demands are being constantly made, it would be quite unrealistic even to envisage a massive programme of textbook translation, to say nothing of the problems of training teachers, and of preparing teaching materials. This is especially so when agencies in France and in the English-speaking world are offering funds and personnel for improving the quality of the Courses given in English and French. In the arts, too, in literature especially, the need for Kenyans, Ghanaians, Ugandans, and Nigerians to have a common medium for the discussion of their problems is acute. At the present time this can be only English or French. In such a climate Swahili does not flourish. In Kenya, and particularly in Uganda, where Colonial language policy favoured the use and development of local languages, English has seemed to offer the best hope for national unity and international co-operation. The recent statement by Uganda's Acting Attorney-General, during the debate on the newly promulgated Constitutional Proposals, if extreme, is perhaps fairly representative:

> . . . official language – that need not delay us. The official language of the Government of Uganda shall be English. Now I hope that people will not spend a large expense of time on asking the Minister of Education when he is going to be teaching Swahili and Zulu: I do not know what other language! We are concerned here only with the Official Language not with teaching another language altogether, which is altogether strange. [Interruption] Yes, if you teach Swahili, you might as well teach Gujerati. Swahili is no nearer to the language of the hon. Member than Gujerati. I want to challenge him on that. No nearer. He might as well learn what they speak in Paraguay as learn Swahili.[2]

But none of these countries is linguistically uni-focal, by which I mean that no one language will serve adequately in all the complex patterns of social, political, and cultural life. If English is the obvious choice for inter-territorial communication some

African language or languages may need to be developed in the interests of national identity, and will surely play an important role in the development of national culture, family life, religion, and even in sport. Uganda recognizes the need to use seven languages at primary-school level and nineteen on the radio; Kenya recognizes that Swahili is – for a large proportion of Nairobi's residents – *the* important language of communication and perhaps also of 'pop' culture; and the Congo gives some official recognition to Swahili, along with three other local languages. Tanzania, however, has gone further than any of her neighbours. She has adopted Swahili as the national language. What this has entailed must be examined in detail.

In the period since independence there has been no dramatic shift in the status of Swahili, indeed in some spheres there has simply been a logical and gradual extension of the areas in which the language was used. What is new is a growing recognition that Swahili is the proper language to use on a large number of occasions on which English would formerly have been used. This is not to minimize the formidable difficulties involved in any major extension in the use of Swahili, but it is now part of Government and Party policy to see that the language is invested with the kind of status which it formerly lacked. Tanzania is still, and is likely to remain, linguistically tri-focal, though the importance of French for contact with francophone Africa adds a new element in the search for opportunities among the *élite*. There is, however, a rather subtle shift in emphasis between the three major areas of language focus. Firstly, English is still the mark of membership in a wider political and economic unit than the State, and with more people enjoying Secondary and Higher education, more English is used. In just what contexts of everyday life English is used in preference to Swahili can only be the subject of guesswork at the present time, but it is clear that it is still the dominant language of the *élite*. Ability to operate only a local language is decreasing, with an increase in educational opportunity, but there is an increasing, if transient, concern on the part of those who are themselves linguistically tri-focal that ties with the local community, and especially their local culture, should not be lost, so that it is not uncommon to find parents who spend much of their time speaking Swahili or English nevertheless teaching their children their own local language. This seems most marked among Haya, Chaga, and Nyakyusa speakers, but it is by no means restricted to them. Where parents belong to different language groups there is no clear propensity to select either the language of the mother or the father. Ability to operate Swahili, however, is now a mark of national pride, even though it may not mean that one operates it any more efficiently than previously, and the choice of Swahili as the national language is in part recognition of the part played by the language during the achievement of independence. On the other hand, it is not easy to say in what specific respects such national pride has contributed to the use of Swahili. There are more frequent letters to the local Press praising the language, perhaps one per fortnight, and there are more poems, perhaps one per month. The following verses are typical of praise-poems occurring:

Mapambo ya Kiswahili, kwa lugha yetu huvuma
Kwa vingi vitandawili, na mashairi kusoma,
Nakutumia methali, na nyimbo za Lelemama
Kiswahili lugha njema, lugha yetu asilia.[3]

(The riches of Swahili are widely known for our language, there are plenty of riddles, and poems to recite; I send you proverbs and songs of the Lelemama dance, Swahili is a good language, our original language.)

Tukitumie kwa haki, karani na wakulima
Na kama hamsadiki, Kingeresa kitahama,
Lugha ngeni hatutaki, twaona zina lawama,
Kiswahili lugha njema, lugha yetu asilia.

(Let us use it as a right, clerks and farmers, and though you may not believe it, English will move out, we don't want foreign languages, we feel they're a reproach, Swahili is a good language, our original language.)[4]

At the same time there has been an increase in societies devoted to the spread and development of the language; informative articles have appeared in the Press, very often concerned with lexical problems and with comparing unfavourably the work of expatriate lexicographers and grammarians with that now being done in such articles. Yet Swahili has been very widely used for the last twenty years, and what one is witnessing now is really a continuing public demonstration of independence, and sentiments such as the following – from a speech by the Minister for Community Development and National Culture – are as much statements of faith as they are programmes for action:

Mr Mgonja said that the language heritage and the study of Kiswahili as a national language was part of the cultural revival. He told the members that Kiswahili was a great national heritage and all was being done to enrich and spread it. He called on people to study the language diligently.[5]

One of the most difficult problems posed by the use of Swahili as a national language is this relationship to the national cultural revival. The great strength of the language in the pre-independence period was the fact that it was associated with no single tribal unit. The culture associated with Swahili, where it does occur as a mother tongue, is generally that of an Islamic coastal community, by no means characteristic of the country as a whole. The national culture of Tanzania is, in a sense, the sum of its regional cultures, expressed in local languages – more than a hundred of them – and tied to local customs and situation. Against such a coastal background such coastal features as the *taarabu* and *magungu* songs are neither more nor less a part of the national culture than is Makonde stilt-dancing.

Bold, far-sighted, and imaginative experiments will need to be made if we are to witness the transformation of regional cultures using local languages into a national culture using Swahili which can command the loyalty, affection, and respect of young Tanzanians.

The two Ministries most closely involved with the development of the language are those of Education and of Community Development and National Culture. The Ministry of Education has for the past few years been paying close attention to the teaching of Swahili at all levels of the educational system.[6] Not only have Workshops (in Mathematics and Science as well as specifically in Swahili) been organized to produce teaching materials at the primary level, but sub-committees have been studying ways of revising the secondary-school syllabus, the form of the School Certificate examination itself, and, most recently, the possibility of extending the teaching of the language up to University entrance level. Not only will pupils entering secondary schools have to satisfy the authorities of their competence in the language but during their four years of Courses leading to the School Certificate, Swahili will be a compulsory subject. Mention should also be made of the fact that Courses in Swahili were introduced at the University College, Dar es Salaam, in 1964 in association with Courses given in descriptive linguistics.

The biggest problems to be faced here are the shortage of trained teachers and teaching materials. This is least acute in the primary schools and most acute at the higher forms of the secondary schools. At this level the teaching of Swahili has suffered from a situation inherited from the pre-independence period when the teaching of the language was often in the hands of expatriates, or teachers who, though trained in another subject, were held for one reason or another to be capable of teaching Swahili. While it is the second language of the great majority of Tanzanians, it received a much smaller weekly allocation of time than does English (3 hours as against 8–9 hours), the disparity between the variety of teaching materials available encouraged the view that the language was somehow inferior, and for many years it constituted an easy option in the School Certificate. For every book available for general reading, ten were forthcoming in English, whose content and variety stimulated students eager to progress to higher education. Too often such Swahili books as have been available have been inherited from lists prescribed for primary schools. While there are at present quite a number of people writing various kinds of material suitable for the primary school, there is virtually no one writing material for secondary schools. This is partly because those in the country who know what is needed at that level are largely committed to English, and partly because those who have both the ability and enthusiasm have not the time. There is, furthermore, very little conception of what is involved in 'grading', it being widely assumed that what is more difficult is that which contains more difficult words.

There is an additional problem at the primary level, where the medium of instruction is Swahili, of translating the technical terms used in scientific subjects. There is no doubt that, given time and resources, this can be done perfectly adequately,[7] the real question is not whether it is possible but, given available resources, whether it is practicable. The possibility of extending the use of Swahili as a medium of instruction into the secondary schools is a somewhat controversial question, but again there is no doubt that it could be done if it were felt that resources could be diverted to it.

From its inception the Ministry of Community Development and National Culture has been concerned with the development of Swahili as an expression of the national culture, and at various times during the past few years plans have been put forward for the establishment of additional organizations to carry out the general task of 'developing the language', though these have usually had to be shelved for lack of funds.[8] With

H

the appointment of a 'Promoter for Swahili' new attempts were made to set up cultural committees throughout the country, which have as one of their aims the task of encouraging people to use Swahili more. A useful summary of the Ministry's views has been given by the Swahili Promoter, Mr S. Mushi, and they are, on the whole, typical of much that has been said, both officially and unofficially, during the past few years:

> The role played by Swahili language in Tanzania is immense. Almost everybody in Tanzania can speak the language: and, therefore, it has become a useful medium of communication. Since the language has now become the national language, we feel we must do something to widen its scope so that it may be sufficiently useful in all Government activities, in schools and commercial circles. We want to rid the language of bad influences and to guide it to grow along the proper road. We want to standardise its orthography and usage, and to encourage all our people to learn to speak and write properly grammatical Swahili.[9]

While one may applaud the sentiments of such a statement, it leaves many points of policy unresolved, and gives no hint as to how such ideals may be translated into reality. What, for example, is meant by 'sufficiently useful'; does it mean that all Government business will be carried out in Swahili, as is being attempted in Zanzibar? Does it mean that instruction in secondary schools should be carried out in Swahili? One must distinguish between long-term and short-term aims. It seems likely that in the long-term it is hoped that ultimately Swahili will be used for all internal State business[10] and that it might even be used as a medium of instruction in secondary schools where this can be shown to be practicable, but in the short-term all that is intended is that efforts should be made to extend the use of the language wherever possible. To this end, for example, the Ministry is trying to compile a list of suitable terms for use within the various Ministries, and it is likely that other lists will be compiled in other fields. However, the only serious work in this field so far has been the attempt to provide a legal dictionary for translating the country's Laws. A Sub-Committee was set up in 1963 by the Minister, the late Sheikh Amri Abedi, under the Chairmanship of Professor A. B. Weston, [11] then Dean of the Faculty of Law, University College, Dar es Salaam. This met regularly between 1963 and 1965, and a preliminary version of the projected dictionary was prepared in a cyclostyled form.[12] This represents a selection of appropriate legal terms culled from various legal dictionaries and initially based on a list prepared by the Minister, from an English–Urdu Law dictionary. This material is now being revised and will then require checking against the legal terms that are actually in use in the lower courts. This project has raised many important questions; should a legal terminology be esoteric and used only by specialists, in which case one may only require of it that lawyers be satisfied as to its definitions and linguists as to the relation between the legal definitions provided and those others which may be in non-specialized use. If, however, one asks that a legal dictionary be accessible to all, then one must assess the implications for various terminologies already in use in the courts of additional requirements embodied in such a dictionary. Refinement of terminology necessarily involves a redefinition of terms within the system under consideration.

Again, what is meant by references to 'bad influences' and the desire to guide the language to grow along the 'proper road'? We do, in this case, know something about people's views on 'bad influences'. Late in 1964 the second Vice-President sent a circular to Civil Servants and others urging them to 'desist from the habit of mixing Swahili and English'. By this is meant particularly the habit of code-switching within a given sentence, e.g. Halafu tulirudi ofisini tukakutana na Bwana X. and had a very fruitful discussion. Then we returned to the office, met Mr X. . . .[13] Criticism was also levelled at the inordinate use of English terms, and Civil Servants were urged to remedy the weakness of 'being unable to express themselves elegantly in Swahili'. Another such influence is that of in-adequate translation, in which the material is either carelessly handled or translated literally from English. A good example of this was cited recently by a correspondent in the daily *Uhuru* of 3 March 1966 from a radio news bulletin:

> Mnasikiliza radio Tanzania kutoka Dar es Salaam. Na sasa mtasomewa hutuba ya Bwana Waziri alio wahutubia wafanya kazi wa pwani *akiwa yeye ni kama Waziri wa Leba*.

> (You are listening to Radio Tanzania from Dar es Salaam. And now you will have read to you the speech of the Minister addressing workers on the coast, *in his capacity of Minister of Labour/as though he were the Minister of Labour*.)

The correspondent draws attention only to the final phrase, which he finds meaningless, but the rest of the citation also bears the mark of literal translation. Another habit which has received widespread criticism is that of the extensive use of loan-words, especially where there do exist already suitable terms in Swahili. Thus, a Mr K. Z. Kidasi, writing in *Uhuru* of 14 March 1966, complains of the use of a word like 'kuinjoy' (English, Enjoy) when perfectly adequate non-loans exist. Criticism of colloquialism seems to be the import of the Minister of Community Development and National Culture's reference (1964) to 'lugha isiyo na asili', which in the newspapers 'leads people into bad habits', and he urged all Swahili newspapers to appoint a language expert to vet all articles – this remark was greeted by cheers – so that they should appear in a manner fit for bequeathing to the next generation.[14] In similar vein, Mr J. K. Kiimbila, writing in *Kiongozi*, urges that Swahili should not be 'destroyed' by the inordinate use of Arabic loans, though his evidence is not really representative.[15] To sum up, then, bad influences appear to comprise code-switching, inordinate use of loans, colloquialisms, and literal translations.

The call to standardize orthography and usage raises different problems again: firstly, it must be pointed out that a very considerable degree of standardization of orthography has already been achieved, particularly in school textbooks and books generally, though it must be admitted that standardization is much less in evidence in some newspapers.[16] On the other hand, it is difficult to know what is meant by a standardization of usage, and there is little guidance from Swahili speakers themselves, who would probably agree that over an area as large as that in which Swahili is spoken, variation of dialect, register, style, and mode[17] are likely to be considerable and, further, as inevitable as they are desirable. It is worth remarking at this point that while there are a considerable number of studies of Swahili dialect, there is virtually nothing on register, style, or mode.

The suggestion that everyone should 'speak and write properly grammatical Swahili' raises a number of questions. First of these is the fact that Swahili is a second language for perhaps 90 per cent of Tanzanians, so that while it is operated with facility by such speakers, there is considerable local variation at all levels. Furthermore, there is, at present, a wide divergence of opinion among those who regard themselves as experts not only as to what is or is not acceptable but also regarding those whose views on 'acceptability' can be accepted. It is worth considering in some detail the views of one such expert, Sh. Mohamed Ali. Writing in the local *Nchi Yetu* (December 1964),[18] he distinguishes three groups of Swahili speakers. The first group comprises those for whom Swahili is a first language and who therefore 'understand Swahili words by recognising all their meanings from within', and are able to differentiate between words of closely similar meaning.[19] Such speakers are, however, not familiar with modern educational and scientific usage. The second group – one might almost say second grade – of speakers are also first-language speakers, but while they speak with fluency, there are limits to the range of their competency, particularly when faced with unaccustomed patterns, such as epigrammatic sayings in dialect.[20] The third group are those for whom Swahili is a second language and they are subdivided into three: the first learned some Swahili at school[21] and then went on to higher education in English. While some of this sub-group make efforts to improve their Swahili, others boast of their skill and try to substitute their own 'rotten' variety of Swahili for others' 'good' Swahili. The second subgroup comprises those who have neither learned Swahili at school nor are interested in learning 'proper' Swahili.[22] Finally, there is a third sub-group, who despite the handicap of having to learn it as a second language, nevertheless apply themselves to the task with diligence and even write books. The '*hubris*' of such speakers is in their assumption of omniscience and their attempts to 'bend' the language according to the logic of their own thoughts without paying complete attention to its 'original' form.[23]

The view put forward here that language competence is somehow bound up with the knowledge of an extensive vocabulary is very widely held and occurs in many discussions on the language, whether one is talking about the need to upgrade examination papers or to raise people's language competence generally. It is, perhaps, bound up with traditions in Swahili versification, where a premium is put on the poet's ability to use such a vocabulary to outwit a poetic rival. One of the objectives of the characteristic Swahili verse-contests, avers a leading Swahili poet, is 'to dive into the sea of the poet's thoughts, so that very few of those who are not poets can understand these contests'.[24]

In addition to the Ministries which are especially concerned with Swahili, some mention must be made of the Institute of Swahili Research and of the various independent organizations which have flourished intermittently. The Institute of Swahili Research was established as a Research Unit of the University College, Dar es Salaam, in 1964[25] with the initial help of a three-year grant from the Ministry of Overseas Development in London and the Calouste Gulbenkian Foundation, together with annual subventions from the Governments of Kenya and the United Republic (£800 from each plus £175 from Zanzibar). Uganda decided, however, to withdraw its support.[26] It thereby absorbed and transformed the East African Swahili Committee which preceded it and whose earlier history has been discussed in the preceding chapter.

The Institute is primarily concerned with basic research into language, literature, and lexicography, and the project to which most of its resources will be devoted over the next few years will be a new Swahili–English dictionary. This is fitting, since the present Standard Swahili dictionary was largely the work of the East African Swahili Committee's first Secretary, and the Committee maintained a close interest in lexicography throughout the period of its life. Indeed, from the many lists of terms which the Committee discussed, drew up, and published was learned the important lesson that you may tell people what they should say, but you cannot effectively persuade them to say it unless you have really massive resources at your disposal. For most of the past fifteen years the Committee had very slender resources, and these were always stretched to the utmost. From the continuing work of the dictionary, which is a long-term project, it is hoped to produce lists of new terms, words not in the present dictionary, etc., with each issue of the *Journal*, and the Institute is also collaborating with the Ministry of Community Development and National Culture. It is also proposed to produce two small dictionaries for schools, one at primary level and one at secondary level. In the field of literature the Institute is interested in facilitating the collection of literary and historical material and, where possible, assisting in the editing of such as can be made available to the general public. A large collection both of manuscripts and microfilm has now been deposited in the Library of the University College, thanks largely to the energies of Dr J. Knappert and Mr J. W. T. Allen and the generosity of the supporting Foundations. It must be stressed, however, that much of the collection is of religious material, and that all of it needs careful and detailed annotation and editing before it can do anything to remedy the acute shortage of books in schools. Language research has been carried on as and when staff were available. Dr E. Closs, while at the University College, made a detailed study of the copula in Swahili, in collaboration with the Institute's two Research Assistants, and the Director, likewise, made an equally detailed study of transitivity and verbal extensions.

During the first five years of independence two independent organizations devoted to Swahili also came into existence, the first representing a continuation of a similar society founded some ten years previously in Tanga. Both have operated fitfully, and their activities are at present (Jan. 1968) suspended while plans are being worked out for their amalgamation.

The Jumuiya ya kustawisha Kiswahili (Association for the Advancement of Swahili) was founded in 1963 and set out its main objectives at the end of 1964. They may be summarized as follows:

(a) To discover the origins of Swahili words, in the belief that understanding the origin of something is to understand its quality, and indeed is the basis for loving and respecting it.[27]

(b) To cherish Swahili, by correcting the misleading use of words.

(c) To co-operate with similar-minded bodies.

(d) To promulgate preferred usage.

(e) To increase the word-stock of the language.

(f) To correct existing grammatical descriptions.

(g) To translate and write books.

These objectives were, as far as possible, pursued mainly by weekly articles in the Press and talks on the radio. The newspaper articles appearing in *Ngurumo* under the title of

'Tengeneza Kiswahili' (See to Swahili) were primarily concerned with common errors, such as the confusion between 'kh' and 'h', or the tendency for some speakers to reproduce 'r' for 'l', or for speakers to use a word with a meaning different from its original meaning.[28] They have also chastised the Institute of Swahili Research for using 'katika' in its title instead of 'wa', apparently forgetting that they had themselves scrutinized the title before it was used. More recently they drew attention to errors in the existing dictionaries.

It is worth pointing out that no one – least of all the authors – is complacent about the serious lacunae in existing grammatical and lexical studies, and it is a pity that societies such as this did not do more in the way of constructive criticism.

The Chama cha usanifu wa Kiswahili na Ushairi (Society for the Enhancement of the Swahili Language and Verse), under the leadership of the leading poet, Mr M. E. Mnyampala, had five main objectives:

1. To preserve the language, encourage its poetry and also purity of form and style: to develop the language in Bantu terms and encourage poetry as a special study which contributes to a knowledge of Swahili for the national benefit.
2. To awaken and stimulate people who wish to be experts in the language and poetry.
3. To awaken the efforts of those who wish to write books on various subjects in Swahili, and in verse, and to find ways of publishing their work.
4. To set about compiling a dictionary and grammar more adequate than the present ones.
5. To encourage dramatic performances, and other cultural features.

The society charged a membership fee of 5s. per year and was said to have several hundred members, mainly in Dar es Salaam, but since it did not receive any financial support from the

Government, its activities were somewhat limited. Like the Jumuiya, it contributed a series of weekly articles, from time to time, in *Uhuru*, entitled *Taaluma ya Kiswahili*, which were mainly concerned with examining words commonly confused, or which are closely similar in meaning, but it also branched out into discussing dialectal variants, names for children's games, birds, animals, and proverbial utterances.

One cannot predict what form these independent organizations will take in the coming years, but there are signs that the Tanzanian Government may try to co-ordinate the various bodies devoted to the propagation and development of Swahili. In August 1967 a National Swahili Council was set up whose functions are defined as:

(*a*) To promote the development and usage of the Swahili language throughout the United Republic.

(*b*) To co-operate with other bodies in the United Republic which are concerned to promote the Swahili language and to endeavour to co-ordinate their activities.

(*c*) To encourage the use of the Swahili language in the conduct of official business and public life generally.

(*d*) To encourage the achievement of high standards in the use of the Swahili language and to discourage its misuse.

(*e*) To co-operate with the authorities concerned in establishing standard Swahili translations of technical terms.

(*f*) To publish a Swahili newspaper concerned with the Swahili language and literature.

(*g*) To provide services to the Government, public authorities, and individual authors writing in Swahili with respect ro the Swahili language.

At the time of writing, however, I have no information on the extent to which these functions have been translated into practical terms.

FURTHER READING

Little has appeared so far on the post-independence period in Africa which has a direct bearing on the substance of this chapter. Two articles only should be noted:

L. HARRIES, 'Swahili in Modern East Africa', being a paper delivered to a Conference on the language problems of developing nations held at Airlie House, Va., in November 1966.

E. POLOMÉ, 'The Position of Swahili and Other Bantu Languages in Katanga', being a paper submitted to the 2nd International Congress of Africanists, Dakar, 11–20 December 1967.

VII · Problems of a National Language

Success in language planning depends on the already existing network of social communication, that is on the established channels of commerce in material and intellectual goods. It matters less with whom one is able to communicate than with whom one wants to communicate.

P. S. RAY, *Language Standardisation*,
Mouton, 1963, pp. 73–4

In discussing the problems of a national language policy, we should, I think, try to be clear about the areas over which the policy applies. Though the United Republic of Tanzania has chosen Swahili as the national language, this does not mean, as I have pointed out already, that Tanzania is linguistically unifocal. For example, in inter-territorial affairs, higher education, the High Court, certain technical fields of government, e.g. medicine, and in post-primary education, at least for the time being, the language of communication is English. By contrast, in the National Assembly, for example, the Party, Trade Unions, the lower courts, the regional administration, primary education, and certain areas of the Civil Service, Swahili is either exclusively or largely used. At home, on the other hand, a much more complex state of affairs obtains. In families where the parents have not been to secondary school at least one local language and Swahili are probably used, with a local language predominating where both parents come from the same language group and/or the language is Haya, Nyakyusa, Chaga, or Gogo, languages to which speakers seem to have a particularly strong allegiance. If the parents come from different language groups, or if the family is living away from their locality of origin as do many Government and Party officials, then Swahili is likely to predominate. With increasing social mobility, increasing literacy, and increasing sophistication of teaching methods with reference to Swahili, this tendency is likely to be reinforced. If one or other or both parents have been to secondary school, then English will probably be added to the languages spoken. We cannot yet identify which social roles are regularly characterized by the use of which language, but from what little we do know, usage is clearly patterned along several different axes.

In other words, the United Republic, with many other countries in the world today, is multi-lingual, with each language fulfilling certain functions. *Mutatis mutandis* we have a situation similar to the one described by Einar Haugen for Norway, 'One of them claims to be the more civilized, the other the more Norwegian.' To the extent that modern states participate in supra-national groupings, e.g. the European or East African Common Market, the Organization of African Unity, the United Nations, etc., then some supra-national language is necessary. In so far as there is a need to establish a national identity for political or cultural reasons, then a national language, in this case Swahili, has an important role to perform. Where local ties are important, to reinforce a sense of continuity with the past, for example, or to affirm the values of a local group at a time when these seem in danger of submersion within a larger unit, then a local language comes to the fore. There is some evidence from outside East Africa that as political and economic units increase in size, so the units which lose their identity politically or economically may assert their cultural identity. An interesting case is provided by the recent history of Welsh, Gaelic, and Irish in Great Britain and Eire, and it would be revealing to know something of the reaction of cultural minorities to membership of the European Common Market.

Within East Africa it was observable that an increasing concern for the Mombasa dialect of Swahili in the early fifties was apparently correlated with an awareness that the future of the dialect was jeopardized by Standard Swahili, not merely through the spread of education but also from the great influx of up-country Kenyans who came to the city looking for work. A similar concern seemed to underlie the activities of the many small language committees which flourished in Kenya and Uganda in the years before independence, and still seems to motivate such organizations as the Rwenzururu movement in Western Uganda and the demand for the teaching of Gisu in the eastern part of the country. One of the most important concerns of these multi-lingual states is the distribution of language loyalties within the state. No one would wish to see these polarized along a scale of prestige, but rather distributed in such a way that each is accorded prestige within its own sphere, each sphere being recognized as having an important role to play within the life of the nation as a whole. However, some tendencies from the Colonial period will need to be corrected, and this may result, in the short run, in Swahili being accorded what might appear to be an exaggerated status, while efforts are being made to equip it to take its place effectively as a national language over as wide an area of the national life as possible.

There are, it seems to me, at least two important aspects to a national language policy: the ideological and the technological. The ideological aspect is concerned with mobilizing the nation's sentiments, and with ensuring that the image of the language is kept in the public eye as much as possible. This may cost relatively little, and can sometimes achieve quite startling results, though these are likely to be ephemeral unless they are quickly and effectively reinforced by technological implementation. As with Hebrew in the nineteenth and Turkish and Chinese in the twentieth centuries, such ideology commonly derives its impetus, and ultimately also its effective implementation, from the efforts of small groups of dedicated chauvinists who may well, in the first instance, be members of an educated *élite*. Writing of recent developments in Modern Standard Chinese (MSC), Paul Kratochvil comments:

> It is important to realize that MSC, as well as any other modern standard language, is necessarily a partly artificial system: beside embodying trends typical for the natural process of language development, it also permits the influence of largely subjective and deliberate acts aimed at the achievement of not wholly linguistic goals. Moreover, it is a system in the formation of which the educated minority plays the most important creative role, . . .[1a]

The technological aspect is concerned with the practical problems of implementing the ideology: with the working out, for example, of new Courses throughout the educational system, with training teachers to teach them, and with devising terminologies for such areas of the national life as are thought to require them and where such have previously been lacking. This is likely to cost much more and to take a much longer period of time, depending as it does on the work of specialists in many fields who may have to be specially recruited or diverted from other activities. In facing up to the challenge of her national language policy, Tanzania is faced with three major problems at the technological level.

The first of these is the educational one, which has already been mentioned in the previous chapter. There is an acute shortage of reading material, which becomes more pronounced, the higher up the educational system one proceeds. There is also a shortage of teachers trained not only in teaching the language but also in the general principles and objectives of second-language teaching as applied to Swahili. Finally, there is a need to modernize the Courses themselves, which do not show the effects of recent research in the way that, for example, the History syllabuses do. No sixth-form courses are yet available to prepare students for study of the language at the University.

The shortage of reading materials can be alleviated, in the short run, only by a massive programme of book production undertaken by people with the necessary qualifications. The possibility of seconding personnel on full salary is a difficult one, partly because there is a widespread shortage of skilled staff generally, and partly because of the expense involved. While it may not be possible to allocate sums of the order of the £30,000 per year that Turkey put into her language programme during the period 1946–9,[2] it is important to remember that the effective implementation of a language policy costs money, and that where resources are scarce, this means delicate decisions as to whether and which resources should be switched. Some increase in the allocation of resources seems essential here.[3]

The second problem is concerned with the devising of technical and specialized terminologies for use in those sectors of the national life for which terms have not hitherto been available. This, also, is a long and costly task. In the preceding chapter I referred to the work of the legal dictionary committee, and this is an excellent example of the kind of effort which needs to be made, over several fields and with the same kind of dedication and enthusiasm which has characterized the work of this committee.[4] In particular, work needs doing on the special concepts of economics and politics. If the country wishes to utilize the resources and enthusiasm of its citizens to the full, then there must be a minimum of misunderstanding of the nature of the political and economic objectives involved in particular policies. Writing some years ago on the problems of trade-union terminology, I commented on the extent to which simplification both of terminology and objective appeared to be a characteristic feature of the literature on the subject.[5]

Both unions and political parties started out as organizations with specific aims and objectives; the former to wage the struggle against the employers for a living wage, and the latter to fight and overthrow colonial governments (the Wabeberu – He-goats). Indeed, the term *chama*, with its well-established denotation of 'guild, association', was used for all organizations with specific aims, thus: *chama cha siasa*, political party; *chama cha ushirika*, Co-operative Society; *chama cha wafanyi (wafanya) kazi*, trade union (lit. workers' association); *chama cha Jazz-Boys*, Jazz Boys' Club; *chama cha mpango wa masomo na uchumi*, (The Gusii) education and welfare association. What distinguished a *chama* from other types of organization such as *jumuia* or *kilabu* (club)[6] is not clear; some have suggested the payment of dues or the existence of officials, but there is little doubt that the proliferation of different kinds of *chama* derived more from analogy with those conspicuously successful organizations, the *chama cha siasa* and the *chama cha wafanyi kazi*, than from any attribute of a *chama* as such. It is worth noting that in the political field the association of a party with quite specific and circumscribed objectives has led to difficulties when the question of an opposition party has been raised. Thus in January 1963 we find Mr O. Odinga arguing in support of President Nyerere's adoption of a one-party system that 'at this time in Africa there are no politics/policies of opposition, rather politics/policies consist in opposing the colonialists and building an African nation',[7] and he was supported by his fellow Kenyan, Mr Mac' Anyengo with 'it is necessary that everything done in Africa be done without (an) opposition'.[8] The other component of the term for a trade union, *wafanyi kazi*, was contrasted in union terminology only with the word for employer(s), since in union thought at the time only two classes of people existed, the workers and the employers. By extension, each tended to be defined contrastively to the other: the workers had to put up with minimal education, low standards of living and wages, and were generally exploited; the employer enjoyed the fruits of his wealth which had been gained at the expense of his labour force. Outside the union field, however, the term could be contrasted with *wasiofanya kazi*, those who don't work, or even with *wakulima*, cultivators, or *wavuvi*, fishermen, where *kufanya kazi* has the connotation of working

I

for wages as against working for oneself. Simplification of issues and objectives was clearly important at the time, and of maximum value when all Tanzanians could be on the same side, as it were. In the years since independence, however, such issues have not always seemed so clear. It may be in the nation's interests not to raise wage levels, and it may be necessary to prohibit strikes. In such circumstances the conceptual framework for unions needs to be more sophisticated if serious contradictions are not to arise. A good example of an important term which is, in my view, already bearing too heavy a connotational load is *uchumi*, economics. The importance of this term to Unions, Party, and Government needs no stressing.

The word is associated with the verbal root -*chum*- which has a primary meaning 'pluck, gather (esp. fruit)', with which it is commonly associated, thus *uchumaji wa buni*, picking coffee; *kuchuma kwa buni*, the picking of coffee. A second meaning, already well established by the early sixties, is that of 'making a profit, carrying on a profitable undertaking', thus, 'We agree that every penny that is made in this country is the rightful property of the man who made it' (tunakubali kwamba kila peni ambalo huchumiwa katika nchi hii ni mali na haki ya yule ambaye amechuma . . . *Mfanyi Kazi*, 4 July 1962) or 'in order to make a profit an employer must get people to work for him' (ili apate kuchuma tajiri inamlazimu awapate watu kumfanya kazi, *Vyama vya Wafanya kazi*, Rashidi M. Kawawa, n.d.). Alongside these meanings, however, is a third, the recent extension to economics and even to commerce, 'The economy of this area depends on coffee' (uchumi wa sehemu hizo umetegemea zao la buni, *Ngurumo*, 13 April 1961). By 1964 some differentiation was noticeable in the contexts associated with these terms. The noun *uchamaji* and the verb -*chum*- appeared to occur with connotations one and two, while the noun *uchumi* occurred with connotation three. *Uchumi*, additionally, had already developed a considerable and interesting range of verbal collocations: for example, one may increase, build, help, drive, promote, raise up, stabilize, make flourish, destroy, and soil the *uchumi*; in its turn the *uchumi* might increase, depend on, continue, and even be available. In at least one context the term is accredited with the power to alter itself, e.g. 'One of the aims of Tanganyika's economy is to broaden the base of the economy . . .' (shabaha mojawapo ya uchumi ni kupanua shina la uchumi, *Ngurumo*, 19 May 1961), and there are numbers of contexts in which it is not clear what kind of an entity the writer conceived the *uchumi* to be. I will cite only two examples of these:

> Remember that it is the banks that drive a country's economy. These banks outside Government control will all look for petty irritations and withdraw, after making their big profit, to go and cry in the shade. [Apropos of the Lombard Banking Corporation's decision to close local branches.]
> . . . because if the economy is not obtainable (?) the first to suffer are the workers since it is they who will be cut [laid off?] so that the economy may continue.

This last makes much better sense if *uchumi* is taken to connote profit-making in the second sense discussed

During 1965 and 1966 I attempted to keep abreast of developments in the usage of this term: a large number of teachers and pupils wrote essays for me, and I noted occurrences in the National Assembly, the Press, and in official publications. I present first a number of extracts from essays by teachers and pupils in which I have relegated the Swahili to footnotes:

1. Many people in this country were able to get their *uchumi* through planting tobacco, coffee, bananas, and maize (Teacher, age 27).
2. When I hear the word *uchumi* I understand it to be the

property or capital which is obtainable in a country to enable it to achieve progress (Teacher, age 23).

3. Its [Tanzania's] *uchumi* is chiefly obtainable through cultivation and mineral resources (Teacher, age 24).

4. The first way we can introduce *uchumi* into our country is through cultivation (Teacher, age 28).

5. Furthermore, passenger buses bring *uchumi*, but if the roads were bad . . . (Teacher, age 25).

6. *Uchumi* is the daily work of a man on his own, or a group of men co-operating together in any job yielding a return (Teacher, age 24).

7. The students with knowledge of *uchumi* who were sent down this year brought loss to the country instead of *uchumi* (Teacher, age 26).

8. *Uchumi* is the capital of your farm or anything which brings you *uchumi* (Pupil, St. VIa).

9. The meaning of *uchumi* is the crops which are planted in your country (Pupil, St. VIa).

10. Many tribes understand how *uchumi* is obtainable and how it is made; many also are making a large *uchumi* by different means to develop their country (Pupil, St.VIa).[9]

This sample represents a fair scatter of the kind of definitions that were provided. In all of them some kind of wealth appears at least to be implicit, whether this is conceived in terms of return on investment (e.g. 1, 3, 6, 8) or as natural resources (e.g. 2, 9). While a clear connection is established between profit as a return for hard work or investment in many cases, examples 4, 5, and 7 are extremely vague, and apart from the connotation of natural resources, it is not easy to see how *uchumi* for individuals is extended to the *uchumi* of the State.

This emerges again very clearly in the course of a speech by the President on 'Uchumi wetu' given to the National Assembly on 13 June 1966, for which both Swahili and English official versions are given.[10] Here it may be necessary to recognize as many as four additional connotations for the term, which is translated in the five following ways:

1. (i) the present economic position (hali yetu ya sasa ya uchumi, p. 2);

 (ii) a fall in our overall economic standards (kupata upungufu katika uchumi wetu, p. 5);

 (iii) for reasons which have nothing to do with the economics of our development (kwa sababu ambazo hazihusiani na uchumi wa nchi yetu, p. 16);

 (iv) so that the public sector of our economy grows alongside the private sector (ili uchumi wa wananchi kwa jumla uendelee sawasawa na uchumi wa matajiri, p. 7).

The Swahili version of this is liable to serious misunderstanding: it could equally well be translated 'so that, in general, profits of ordinary people should keep pace with those of employers'.

 (v) The N.D.C. will only be able to expand the Government-owned sector (i.e. of the economy) as fast as it is given money to do so (N.D.C. inaweza tu kuongeza uchumi wa wananchi kama watapata fedha, p. 7);

2. (i) in terms of constant prices our national income increased by almost 2 per cent (bei zisingeshuka uchumi wetu ungeongezeka 2 kwa mia, p. 5);

3. (i) The Gross Domestic Product (Kiasi cha Uchumi wa Nchi, p. 5);

4. (i) we can therefore increase the amount of money issued when the production of goods increases (kwa hiyo tunaweza kuongeza noti, ikiwa tu uchumi wa nchi umeongezeka, p. 20);

 (ii) further, we have to concentrate our expenditure on those fields which are directly productive (kadhalika hatuna budi kutumia fedha zetu katika kazi zile ambazo zinaleta uchumi, p. 17).

Comparison might be made here to Section (*h*) of the TANU 'creed' from the Arusha Declaration[11] '. . . the State must have effective control over the principal means of production' (Serikali lazima iwe na mamlaka kamili juu ya njia muhimu za kuukuza uchumi).

5. (i) If such things are obtained, then investment can be made without present sacrifice (kama misaada ya namna hiyo ikipatikana, basi uchumi unaweza kuong-ezeka bila ya kujinyima kwa wakati huu, p. 12).

This is a somewhat difficult example, since the Swahili version does not obviously tie in with the English. In the passage preceding the sentence quoted, reference is made to the fact that you can invest money without reducing your current rate of spending only if you can get a loan or gift. *Uchumi* here appears to mean not investment so much as funds available for investment or for anything else.

These examples seem to me to be sufficient to demonstrate that the term *uchumi* is carrying too heavy a burden at a time when clarity of exposition is of particular importance. Without going into the question of possible mistranslations, e.g. 1 (iii), several labels are exemplified:

(*a*) the economy, in whole or in part, e.g. *uchumi wa wananchi* 1 (*iv*);
(*b*) the national income;
(*c*) the gross domestic product;
(*d*) production or productive capacity – this comes close to the second connotation discussed earlier of 'making a profit';
(*e*) resources or funds available for investment.

From these two major areas of meaning seem to stand out: on the one hand, *uchumi* is seen as return or profit on investment of one kind or another; while on the other, it is seen as what may lead to profit, i.e. production, investment, etc. To which of these areas the *uchumi* of the country as a whole is affiliated is not clear, but some clarification of this complex situation seems essential.[12] To these should be added the first meaning discussed, that of 'plucking, gathering', which is still common.

I have spent some time discussing this term because I think it illustrates the kind of situation which is liable to develop during a period of rapid linguistic and political change. The intricacies of modern economic problems cannot be simplified beyond a certain point, and the language needs to be equipped to handle the necessary range of concepts in an unambiguous manner. For this, specialized committees need to be established in which economist and linguist, native speakers of English and Swahili, can work out a viable terminology.

The last technological problem I want to discuss here concerns the literary status of Swahili. I have already mentioned the acute shortage of reading materials for schools, and this is by no means restricted to the educational field. The number of books for the general reader to have come out during the last few years has been no more than a trickle in response to the repeated requests for material by local and expatriate publishing houses. It is somewhat ironical that it is from Kenya, the East African Publishing House, that the strongest flow has stemmed. Clearly this is not a situation that can change overnight; as I pointed out in Nairobi in December 1965:

Reading for pleasure is a habit not easily acquired nor widely practised where no tradition exists, where reading is associated with educational courses for specific ends, and where per capita income is extremely low. But we cannot expect writers to emerge if they cannot be sure of selling their work in sufficient quantities for them to make some profit.[13]

This is not to say that the scene is completely bare: until his tragic death in 1962 Shaaban Robert was undoubtedly Swahili's leading writer, with many prose and verse works to his credit,

Of a slightly younger generation are M. E. Mnyampala, a distinguished poet and writer of prose; K. H. A. Akilimali Snowwhite, the poet, and Mohammed Said Abdullah, the Zanzibar writer of detective stories, perhaps the most gifted prose writer in the language. Yet, great as the achievements of these writers are, there is one respect in which their contributions are limited: they write and continue to write in Swahili not from choice but from necessity. In this respect President Nyerere's translation of *Julius Caesar* is of greater significance. As a young Tanzanian said to me proudly, 'He could just as well have written in English, but he preferred to write in Swahili!' This is the kind of prestige that Swahili needs. But where are the young writers?[14] There is no sign of any prose literature from the younger generation to match the rise of local writers in English: anthologies of East African writing appear in English – prose, drama, and verse – but nothing comparable is in sight for Swahili. Can it be that national horizons are too restricted for young writers? The importance for the future of Swahili of capturing and holding the allegiance of the educated minority cannot in my view be over-estimated. Most people in Tanzania will receive only primary education for a long time; they know that the fortunate few who go on will receive education in a world language, yet they are constantly being exhorted to perfect their use of the national language. If they are not to look down on their hardly won heritage they must receive encouragement from those who, fortunate enough to control a supra-national language, yet choose to write in Swahili. The language has come a long way from the coastal trade, which perhaps it did much to create, and which in turn supported it and carried it abroad. Whether it now emerges as Africa's most virile language, supporting a full educational programme, a mastery over modern technology, and a creative literature, or whether it returns to the coast only time and its speakers can tell.

FURTHER READING

GENERAL AND THEORETICAL STUDIES ON MULTI-LINGUALISM, LANGUAGE STANDARDIZATION, LANGUAGE PLANNING, ETC.

There is a very large and rapid growing bibliography in these fields, and the serious student should consult one of the bibliographies devoted specifically to such topics:

S. S. HARRISON, *The Most Dangerous Decades: an Introduction to the comparative study of language policy in multi-lingual states*, Language and Communication Research Center, Columbia University, 1957, Appendix C, pp. 37–102.

A. PIETRZYK (ed.), *Selected Titles in Sociolinguistics*, Center for Applied Linguistics, Washington, D.C., 1964.

Shorter bibliographies are to be found in Weinreich (1964) and Haugen 1966(*a*), for which see below.

CCTA/CSA, *Symposium on Multilingualism* (Brazzaville, 1962), Pub. No. 87, 1964.

C. FERGUSON, 'Diglossia', *Word*, Vol. 15, 1959, 325–40.

JOSHUA A. FISHMAN, 'Language Maintenance and Language Shift as a Field of Inquiry', *Linguistics*, Vol. 9, 1964, 32–70.

—— 'Who Speaks what Language to Whom and When?', *La Linguistique*, Vol. I, 1965, 67–89.

—— *Language Loyalty in the United States*, Mouton, 1966.

E. HAUGEN, 'Linguistics and Language Planning', *Sociolinguistics*, ed. W. Bright, Mouton, 1966(*a*), pp. 50–67.

R. B. LE PAGE, *The National Language Question*, O.U.P., 1964.

A. FRANK RICE (ed.), *Study of the Role of Second Languages*, CAL, 1962.

P. S. RAY, *Language Standardization*, Mouton, 1963.

JOHN SPENCER (ed.), *Language in Africa*, Cambridge, 1963. See also the review article by I. Fodor, 'Linguistic Problems and "Language Planning" in Africa', *Linguistics*, Vol. 25, 1966, 18–33.

U. WEINREICH, *Languages in Contract*, Mouton, 1964.

CASE STUDIES (See also *Monograph Series on Language and Linguistics*, 15, Georgetown, 1962)

S. R. ALISJAHBANA, *Indonesian Language and Literature: Two Essays*, Cultural Report Series, No. 11, Yale, 1962.

HAIM BLANC, 'The Growth of Israeli Hebrew', *Middle Eastern Affairs*, Vol. 5, 1954, 385–92.

RAM GOPAL, *Linguistic Affairs of India*, Asia Publishing House, London, 1966.

E. HAUGEN, *Language Conflict and Language Planning*, Harvard, 1966(*b*).

U. HEYD, *Language Reform in Modern Turkey*, Oriental Notes and Studies, No. 5, Jerusalem, 1954.

C. O'HUALLACHAIN, 'Bilingualism in Education in Ireland', Report of the 13th Annual Round Table Meeting on Linguistics and Language Studies, *Monograph Series on Language and Linguistics*, 15, Georgetown, 1962, 75–84.

W. R. JONES, 'Attitude towards Welsh as a Second Language', *Brit. J. of Educ. Psych.* (Gen. Sect.), Vol. 19, 1949, 44–52.

G. KELLEY, 'The Status of Hindi as a lingua franca', *Sociolinguistics*, ed. W. Bright, Mouton, 1966, 299–305.

PAUL, KRATOCHVIL, *The Chinese Language To-day*, Hutchinson, 1968.

S. MORAG, 'Planned and Unplanned Development in Modern Hebrew', *Lingua*, Vol. 8, 1959, 247–63.

Report of the Official Language Commission, 1956, Government of India Press, 1957.

Report of the Royal Commission on Bilingualism and Biculturalism: Book I: The Official Languages, Queen's Printer, Ottawa, 1967.

SPECIAL STUDIES RELATING TO SWAHILI

C. M. M. SCOTTON, 'Some Swahili Political Words', *J.M.A.S.*, Vol. III, 4, 1965.

W. H. WHITELEY, 'Political Concepts and Connotations', *St Antony's Papers No. 10*, Chatto and Windus, 1961, 7–21.

—— 'Problems of a lingua franca: Swahili and the Trade Unions', *J.A.L.*, Vol. 3, 3, 1964, 215–25.

—— 'Loanwords in Linguistic Description: a Case Study from Tanzania', East Africa', *Approaches in Linguistic Methodology*, eds. I. Rauch and C. T. Scott, Wisconsin, 1967, 125–43.

Some idea of the meaning of such an important term as '*Ujamaa*' which is currently translated as 'socialism' can be gained from a perusal of:

J. K. NYERERE, *Ujamaa: the Basis of African Socialism*, TANU, 1962.

—— *Ujamaa vijijini*, Mpiga chapa wa Serikali, 1967. (English edition under the title *Socialism and Rural Development*.)

KENYA GOVERNMENT, *African Socialism and its Application to Planning in Kenya*, Government Printer, 1965. (A Swahili version under the title *Ujamaa wa kiafrika*, EAPH, 1965.)

Notes

CHAPTER I

1. J. L. KRAPF, *Outline of the Elements of the Kisuaheli Language*, Tübingen, 1850, pp. 8–9.
2. The terms first, second, and third language refer to the sequence in which they were acquired: a person's first language is thus what is commonly referred to as his 'mother tongue'. The terms primary, secondary, and tertiary, on the other hand, refer to the degree of importance which a language has for a given speaker in his daily life. Thus, a man's first language may be Welsh, while his primary language is English.
3. The prefixed element chi- or ki- designates, in this context, the language.
4. In the standard orthography the sequence *ng'* represents the sound of the velar nasal, the *ng* in the English singing, for example.
5. See the *Kenya Weekly News*, 23 December 1955.
6. The two examples can be translated as follows: (1) Put the scones in the oven and bring the tea-pot. (2) Bring something like a banana only round. What was wanted was an apple!
7. A. WERNER, 'The Wa-Hadimu of Zanzibar', *JAS*, Vol. XV, 1915/6, 356–60.
8. Reported in the *East African Standard*, 6 December 1952.
9. *African Education*, A study of educational policy and practice in British Tropical Africa. The Nuffield Foundation and the Colonial Office, Oxford, 1953, p. 82.
10. *Report of the East Africa Royal Commission*, 1953–5, H.M.S.O., Cmd. 9475, 1955, p. 184.
11. JOYCE CARY, *The Case for African Freedom*, Secker and Warburg, 1944, p. 126.
12. SHAABAN ROBERT, *Pambo la Lugha*, Witwatersand, 1948, pp. 27–31. Compare this with the poem of Samuel Daniel, quoted at the end of Chapter V.
13. Leading article in *The Nationalist*, 1 August 1966.
14. SIR DAUDI CHWA, KABAKA of BUGANDA in the *Uganda News*, 22 February 1929.

15. MARCIA WRIGHT, 'Swahili Language Policy, 1890–1940', *Swahili*, Vol. 35/1, 1965, p. 42.

16. JAN KNAPPERT, *Traditional Swahili Poetry*, Leiden, 1967, p. 3.

17. Op. cit. (1967), p. 9.

18. *Utendi* is the northern dialect form; *utenzi* the southern.

19. LYNDON HARRIES, *Swahili Poetry*, Clarendon, 1962, p. 25.

20. Op. cit. (1967), p. 11.

21. W. HICHENS (ed.), *Diwani ya Muyaka bin Haja el-Ghassaniy*, Witwatersrand, 1940, p. 78.

22. The poem is reproduced – along with others of this genre – in *Al-Akida and Fort Jesus, Mombasa*, Mbarak Ali Hinawy, Macmillan, 1950, p. 44.

23. From 'Why Come Ye Not to Court?', *The Complete Poems of John Skelton*, ed. Philip Henderson, Dent, 1959, p. 330.

24. HEMED BIN SEFU SUMAILI GANDO, from a manuscript collection in my possession.

25. H. U. AMEIR (Kamisaa) in *Uhuru*, 20 October 1967.

26. MOHAMED KHAMIS MUGHERI (LISAAD), from a manuscript collection in my possession.

CHAPTER II

1. *The Nationalist*, 10 July 1967.

2. 'Among the islands of Djawaga dealt with in the present section is that of Andjaba, whose chief town is called – in the language of Zanguebar – Ungudya, and whose inhabitants, though mixed, are at present largely Muslims . . . the staple food being bananas. There are five varieties, thus, those known as *kundi*, *fili*, whose weight may sometimes reach 12 oz, *omani*, *muriyani*, *sukari*.' (My translation.) *Relations de Voyages et Textes Geographiques relatif à l extrême Orient*, Tr. G. Ferrand, Vol. I, Paris, 1913, pp. 174–5.

3. C. SACLEUX, *Dictionnaire Swahili–Français*, Vol. I, 1939, Paris, p. 371.

4. M. GUTHRIE, 'Some Developments in the Pre-history of the Bantu Languages', *J. of African History*, Vol. III, 2, 1962, 273–82.

5. 'The Problem of the Bantu Expansion', *J. of African History*, Vol. VII, 3, 1966, 361–76. This article should be read in conjunction with Merrick Posnansky's 'Bantu Genesis – Archaeological Reflexions', *J. of African History*, Vol. IX, 1, 1968, 7–12.

6. 'To return to the Zendjs and their kings, the name of the king in

this country is *Waklimi*, which means "son of the supreme Lord" ... They give to God the name of *Maklandjalou* which means roughly "sovereign Master" ... but their staple food is a grain (millet?) and a plant called *kalari* which one digs up like truffles.' (My translation.) C. B. de Meynard and P. de Courteille, *Les Prairies d'Or*, Paris, 1861, Vol. III, pp. 29–30. No satisfactory edition of Mas'udi's text is at present available. It is interesting to compare the translation in Guillain (*vide* 10 below): 'Le titre du roi des Zendj,c'est Oklimen, ce qui veut dire le fils du grand maître, c'est-à-dire le dieu du ciel et de la terre: ils appellent le créateur Tamkalandjalou. ...'

7. G. S. P. FREEMAN-GRENVILLE, 'Medieval Evidences for Swahili', *Swahili*, Vol. 29/1, 1959, 10–23. In fairness to Dr Freeman-Grenville, it should be pointed out that the interpretations which I am criticizing were put forward nearly ten years ago, and that he has substantially revised his views since that time. They are cited here merely as examples of the kind of problem that historians of Swahili have to face.

7ᵃ. In an at present unpublished 'Some Notes on Swahili Words and Names in Mas'udi'.

7ᵇ. Op. cit. (unpublished).

8. The discussion of these, and various other, terms occurs in G. S. P. Freeman-Grenville, *The Medieval History of the Coast of Tanganyika*, O.U.P., 1962(*a*), pp. 83, 117.

9. S. A. STRONG, 'The History of Kilwa', *J. of the Asiatic Society*, 1895, p. 388.

10. 'I went on board in the town of Mogadishu, heading for the country of the Swahili (coasts/coastlines) and for the town of Kilwa, in the country of the Zenj. We arrived at the large island of Mombasa, two days by sea from the land of the Swahili. ... The inhabitants (of Mombasa) do not practise agriculture but import grain from the Swahili.' (My translation.) M. Guillain (ed.), *Documents sur l'histoire, la géographie et la commerce de l'Afrique orientale*, Vol. I, Paris, 1857, pp. 291–2. This translation is substantially the same as that of C. Defrémery and B. R. Sanguinetti in their *Voyages d'Ibn Batoutah*, Paris, 1884, p. 191, and as the recent English translation of H. A. R. Gibb.

11. As presented by G. S. P. Freeman-Grenville in his *The East African Coast*, Clarendon, 1962(*b*), p. 131.

12. Freeman-Grenville, op. cit. (1962b), p. 130.

13. Freeman-Grenville, op. cit. (1962b), pp. 146–51.

14. *Purchas his Pilgrimes*, London, 1614 (2nd edn.), Book VII, p. 685.

15. Cited by SIR JOHN GRAY in 'Portuguese Records Relating to the Wasegeju', *Tanganyika Notes*, 29, 1950, 95–6. I have not yet been able to confirm this reference.
16. G. S. P. FREEMAN-GRENVILLE, *The French at Kilwa Island*, Clarendon, 1965, p. 78.
17. FREEMAN-GRENVILLE, op. cit. (1965), p. 80.
18. FREEMAN-GRENVILLE, op. cit. (1965), p. 106
19. FREEMAN-GRENVILLE, op. cit. (1965), p. 222.

CHAPTER III

1. I am using the text as reproduced by L. HARRIES in his *Swahili Poetry*, Clarendon, 1962, pp. 209–10.
2. Quoted by SIR JOHN GRAY in his *History of Zanzibar*, O.U.P., 1962, p. 151. The debt I owe to his history of the island is manifest in these pages, as also to his article in *Tanganyika Notes and Records*, 49, 1957, 'Trading Expeditions from the Coast to Lakes Tanganyika and Victoria before 1857'.
3. M. GUILLAIN, *Documents sur l'histoire, la géographie et le commerce de l'Afrique Orientale*, II, Paris, 1851, p. 408.
3ª. R. BURTON, *Zanzibar: City, Island and Coast*, Vol. II, 1872, p. 408.
4. *Maisha ya Hamed bin Muhammed, yaani Tippu Tip* (Trs. W. H. Whiteley), Supplement to Vols. 28/2 and 29/1 of the *Journal of the East African Swahili Committee*, 1958/9, pp. 75/77.
5. C. VELTEN, *Desturi za Wasuaheli*, Göttingen, 1903, pp. 238–40.
6. MR MACQUEEN, 'Notes on African Geography', *JRGS*, Vol. XV, 1845.
7. R. F. BURTON, *Zanzibar: City, Island and Coast*, Vol. I, London, 1872, p. 438.
8. H. SALT, *A Voyage to Abyssinia and Travels*, London, 1814, Appendix I.
9. Reproduced in C. P. RIGBY, 'Remarks on the North-east Coast of Africa and the Various Tribes by Which it Is Inhabited', *Transactions of the Bombay Geographical Society*, Vol. 6, 1844.
10. J. ROSS BROWNE, *Etchings of a Whaling Cruise*, London, 1846, pp. 575–9.
11. GUILLAIN, op. cit., pp. 479–523.
12. R. F. BURTON, *Sindh*, London, 1851, Appendix IV, pp. 372–4.
13. E. STEERE, *A Handbook of the Swahili Language*, London, 1870 pp. iii–iv.

14. Quoted in Roland Oliver, *The Missionary Factor in East Africa*, Longmans, 1952, p. 79.

15. STEERE, op. cit., p. iv.

16. H. W. WOODWARD, *Collections for a Handbook of the Boondéi Language*, S.P.C.K., 1882, Introduction, p. iv.

CHAPTER IV

1. I owe this quotation to Dr J. Iliffe of the University College, Dar es Salaam.

2. HEMEDI BIN ABDALLAH BIN SAID EL BUHRIY, trs. J. W T. ALLEN, *Utenzi wa Vita vya Wadachi kutamalaki Mrima*, Supplement to *Journal of the East African Swahili Committee*, Vol. 25, 1955 (verses 232–41), p. 33.

3. C. VELTEN, 'Suaheli-Gedichte', *Mitteilungen des Seminars für Orientalische Sprachen*, XX–XXI, 1918.

4. ABDUL KARIM BIN JAMALIDDINI, trs. W. H. WHITELEY, *Utenzi wa Vita vya Maji-Maji*, Supplement to *Journal of the East African Swahili Committee*, Vol. 27, 1957 (verses 24–7), p. 35.

5. In an interesting article by G. Hornsby, 'German Educational Achievement in East Africa', *Tanganyika Notes*, 62/3, 1964, the date 1892 is given (p. 85).

6. W. O. HENDERSON, '(I) German East Africa: 1884–1918', *History of East Africa*, Vol. II, eds. Vincent Harlow, E. M. Chilver, Clarendon 1965, 123–62.

7. The figures are taken from Hornsby, op. cit., who warns against too literal an interpretation of them (p. 87.)

8. Raum, (see p. 77), gives a circulation figure of 800 for 1908, but the copy in my possession labelled 'Mwaka wa 1, Nr. 1' bears the date January 1910.

9. HORNSBY, op. cit., p. 89.

10. Cited by R. L. Buell, *The Native Problem in Africa*, Macmillan, 1928, Vol. I, p. 478.

11. See Chapter V for a detailed discussion of Standard Swahili.

12. Though there is little direct evidence for this from the newspapers of the time, other, perhaps, than from their number and success.

13. Especially from the team of specialists sent out by the Nuffield Foundation. See *African Education: a Study of Educational Policy and Practice in British Tropical Africa*, O.U.P., 1953, pp. 79–84.

14. From 1954 dates the *Kitabu cha maelezo ya kazi ya Mabaraza ya Wenyeji*, Govt. Printer, Dar es Salaam, and work was put in hand

to translate a number of Ordinances and other legal materials, e.g. the *Kitabu cha Nikahi* (1959).

15. For a study of the implications of the use of Swahili as a political language see my 'Political Concepts and Connotations', *St Antony's Papers, 10*, Chatto and Windus, 1961, 7–21.

16. Though from 1930 onwards Kenya contributed about £700 towards the Inter-Territorial Language (Swahili) Committee. See Chapter V.

17. 'The Progress and Problems of the East African Protectorate', *Journal of the Royal Colonial Institute*, Vol. 37, 1906.

18. *Joint Select Committee on Closer Union in East Africa* (Minutes of Evidence), H.M.S.O., 1931. There are numerous references to this matter passim.

19. Note the opening speech of the Governor to Legislative Council in October 1929, '. . . Government is also most anxious to increase the study of the vernaculars. That is the only road to the true understanding of African habits and feelings.' Proceedings of Legislative Council (Third Session), 1929.

20. For a general comment on this see JOHN ROBERTS, 'Kenya's Pop Music', *Transition*, Vol. 19, 1965, 40–3: for a specialized study of the art of a popular Congo artist see DAVID RYCROFT, 'The Guitar Improvisations of Mwenda Jean Bosco', *African Music*, Vol. 2, 2, 1961, 81–98.

21. GEORGE BENNETT and CARL ROSBERG, *The Kenyatta Election: Kenya, 1960–1961*, O.U.P., 1961, p. 135.

22. *Joint Select Committee on Closer Union in East Africa*, Minutes of Evidence, Vol. II, H.M.S.O., 1931, p. 554.

23. *East Africa Royal Commission 1953–5 Report*, Cmd. 9475, H.M.S.O., 1955, p. 184.

24. *Proceedings of the Legislative Council*, Part III, 40th Session, 1960, pp. 1225–9.

25. *Policy statement*, Uganda Peoples Congress, Kampala, 1960, para. 72.

26. E. DE JONGHE, 'Les langues littéraires communes au Congo: Kiswahili, Lingala, Kikongo, Kiluba', *XI Semaine de Missiologie*, Louvain, 1933, p. 69.

27. DE JONGHE, op. cit., p. 72.

28. E. DE JONGHE, 'L'Unification des langues congolaises', *B. des Séances Inst. Roy. Col. Belge*, Vol. XV, 2, 1944, pp. 274–5.

29. V. GELDERS, 'La langue commune au Congo', *B.I.R.C.B.*, Vol. XV, 2, 1944, pp. 286–313.

30. E. POLOMÉ, 'Cultural Languages and Contact Vernaculars in the

Republic of the Congo', *Studies in Literature and Language*, University of Texas, Vol. IV, 4, 1963, p. 503.

31. L. HARRIES, 'Swahili in the Belgian Congo', *Tanganyika Notes*, 39, 1955, 13.

32. G. VAN DER KERKEN, 'Le Swahili, langue de grande expansion', *B.I.R.C.B.*, Vol. XV, 2, 1944, 260–1.

33. L. HARRIES, 'Congo Swahili', *Tanganyika Notes*, 44, 1956, 50–3.

34. HARRIES, op. cit. (1955), p. 14.

35. Personal communication from J. W. T. Allen.

36. Personal communication from G. S. P. Freeman-Grenville.

CHAPTER V

1. The version of the poem which appears in R. A. SNOXALL, 'How Swahili is Changing', *Bulletin of the East African Inter-Territorial Language (Swahili) Committee* (B.I.T.L.C.), Vol. 21, 1951, p. 8, has two additional lines.

2. Quoted by B. J. Ratcliffe in the 'History, Purpose and Activities of the Inter-Territorial Language Committee', *B.I.T.L.C.*, Vol. 16, 1942. For the early history of the Committee I have leaned heavily on this article, as also on the files of the Committee for this period.

3. J. L. KRAPF, *A Dictionary of the Swahili Language*, London, 1882, p. x.

4. 'Modern Swahili', *B.I.T.L.C.*, Vol. 7, 1934, 3–10.

5. 'An Answer by Canon Broomfield to the Memorandum Modern Swahili', *B.I.T.L.C.*, Vol. 7, 1934, p. 18.

6. Op. cit., p. 19.

7. Op. cit. (Modern Swahili), p. 6.

8. Editorial to *B.I.T.L.C.*, Vol. 22, 1952.

9. See the Annual Report of the Committee for 1952–3. The revised methods by which the Committee worked involved the deletion of items v, vii, viii, and xi, and the modification of iii as set out in the earlier Constitution on p. 3.

10. See the discussion of this Meeting in *B.I.T.L.C.*, Vol. 21, 1951, pp. 17–18.

11. These *Bulletins* appeared at least annually until 19 of 1945. Thereafter 20 appeared in 1947, 21 in 1951, and 22 in 1952.

12. Annual Report of the Committee 1952–3, p. 2.

13. Quinquennial Report of the Committee, 1952–7, p. 5. In this

K

Report is included the revisions of the Constitution consequent upon the move to Makerere.

14. *The Poetical Essayes of Sam. Danyel*, London, 1599.

15. *Mulcaster's Elementarie*, ed. with an Introduction by E. T. Campagnac, Clarendon, 1925, pp. 274–5.

CHAPTER VI

1. This is discussed in some detail in Ali A. Mazrui, 'The English Language and Political Consciousness in British Colonial Africa', *J.M.A.S.*, Vol. 4, 3, 1966.

2. *Uganda Parliamentary Debates (Hansard)*, 2nd Series, Vol. 72, 1967–8, p. 330.

3. It is worth comparing this with the well-known poem of the late Shaaban Robert written nearly twenty years ago:

   Swahili is rich, in its elegance and proverbs, and I think that in the near future, it will be possible to translate many fields of education, and render a service to mankind both with insight and beauty, mother's breast is sweet, no other satisfies. *Pambo la Lugha*, Witwatersrand, 1948.

2. JUMA SHAMTE MAKUKA, 'Kiswahili lugha njema', *Uhuru*, 16 July 1966.

5. Reported in *The Nationalist* of 27 June 1966. It is worth drawing attention here to the language programme of Turkey in the period 1920–50, which in some ways paralleled that of Tanzania. Note the characteristic tone in the statutes of the Constitution of the Turkish Linguistic Society (1932), that the aim of the Society was 'to bring out the genuine beauty and richness of the Turkish language and to elevate it to the high rank it deserves among world languages.' U. Heyd, *Language Reform in Modern Turkey*, Oriental Notes and Studies No. 5, Jerusalem, 1954, pp. 25–6.

6. See, for example, the speech of the Minister of Education presenting his estimates for 1963/4, *Hansard*, 7th Meeting, 1963, pp. 710–35.

7. Some idea of what can be done in this field is provided by Mohamed Hyder in his 'Swahili in a Technical Age', *East Africa's Cultural Heritage*, Contemporary African Monographs Series, No. 4, E.A.P.H., 1966. (Referred to subsequently as *EACH*.)

8. Such as that for establishing a special magazine to serve as a means of presenting models of Swahili prose and verse and of disseminating results of research. This was mentioned in the

Estimates of the Ministry of National Culture and Youth for 1963/4 (*Hansard*, 7th Meeting, Govt. Printer, 1963, p. 946) and again in the estimates of the Ministry of Community Development and National Culture of 1964/5 (*Hansard*, 13th Meeting, Govt. Printer, 1964, p. 874), but still not implemented. See a similar proposal put forward by the Chama cha usanifu wa Kiswahili in *Uhuru*, 22 February 1966.

9. 'The Role of the Ministry of Culture in National Development', presented to a seminar on African culture and new writing held in Nairobi 2–7 December 1965 and subsequently published in *EACH*, p. 18.

10. A Circular from the Second Vice-President of 1964 refers to a time when 'kazi zetu zote na za kila namna zitaendeshwa kwa Kiswahili' and a second statement, of 4 January 1967 has directed that Swahili be used for all Government business, and that the use of English or any other foreign languages unnecessarily is to cease forthwith. All Ministries, District Councils, Co-operative Unions, and parastatal organizations are therefore obliged to use Swahili in their day-to-day business.

11. A useful statement of the problems involved is Professor A. B. Weston's 'Law in Swahili – a Problem in Developing the National Language', *East African Law Journal*, Vol. 1/1, 1965.

12. At the same time a small translation unit in the Ministry of Justice has been working on the Penal Code and other projects. It would be wrong, however, to imagine that this is the first time that legal translation has been instituted. Reference has been made in Chapter IV to the work done in the fifties, which included also the Explosives Ordinance, *Sheria na Kanuni ya vita vya kalipuka*, Govt. Printer, 1959. Recent work includes the *Sheria za Mahakama za Mahakimu (1963)*, Govt. Printer, 1963; the *Maelezo ya Mahakama za Mwanzo*, 1964; and the Standing Rules for the National Assembly, *Kanuni za Bunge la Taifa*, 1966.

13. I have discussed this and similar phenomena in my 'Loan-words in Linguistic Description; a Case Study from Tanzania', *Approaches in Linguistic Methodology*, eds. I. Rauch and C. T. Scott, Univ. of Wisconsin Press, 1967.

14. *Hansard*, 13th Meeting (16 June–3 July), 1964, pp. 874–5. 'Ingefaa magazeti yote ya Kiswahili yaweke fundi lugha ambaye atasahihisha makala zote ili – (makofi) – zitokee kwa lugha safi itakayofaa kurithiwa na watoto wetu.'

15. Neither he nor other opponents of the use of Arabic loans reach the extremes of the early Turkish linguistic nationalists.

'... even the most uncouth Turkish word ... is to us more pleasing than the most harmonious foreign word.' On the other hand, Tanzanians do not always recognize the truth of the position later adopted by the Turkish Linguistic Society in 1945, 'We have no right to impose words. We make them and the Government and the writers use them if they want to.' Heyd, op. cit., pp. 30, 53.

16. A reminder of the rules originally agreed on in 1926, together with some recent comments appears in *Swahili*, Vol. 36/1, 1966, pp. 11–14.

17. I am following here the terminology of J. C. Catford in his *A Linguistic Theory of Translation*, O.U.P., 1965.

18. His views were challenged by J. K. Kiimbila and others in a series of articles in *Kiongozi* during May and June 1966 entitled 'Kiswahili si lugha ya kabila fulani'.

19. He cites as evidence the following series of words which all might be translated by the English term 'fool': *zuzu*, a 'greenhorn'; *zebe*, a 'half-wit'; *mpumbavu*, a stupid person; *bahau*, a 'bullish', unintelligent person; *duwazi*, a simpleton; and *mjinga*, an ignoramus, a really stupid person.

20. He selects for this 'ndimiye mzushi mabaa. Kwambawe si mtambuzi wa lo ndimi mjulishawe.'

21. '... limekujua kiswahili mitaani tu au limepata kujua kiswahili katika shule kwa kuparuza tu.'

22. '... hawajishughulishi na kutaka kukijua kiswahili kama ipasavyo.'

23. 'Ubaya wao ni kuwa hujaribu sana kukiviringa Kiswahili kwa mujibu wa fikira zao bila kuangalia kwa utimilifu umbile lake la asili.' In this article as in the correspondence mentioned above, Sh. Mohamed Ali shows himself to be a Platonist e.g. maneno ya lugha yo yote huwa kila neno lina maana yake maalum iliyowekewa neno hilo toka kuanzishwa kwake, *Kiongozi*, 1 June 1964, p. 12, while Mr Kiimbila, perhaps as a result of his year's course in Linguistics in the United States, maintains a more Aristotelian view of the meaning of words and change of meaning, thus, note his criticism of Sh. Mohamed Ali and others who ' ... hufikiri kuwa maadam neno fulani lilikuwa na maana fulani wakati wa miaka nenda na miaka rudi, basi maana yake hubakia ile ile', *Kiongozi*, 15 March 1964.

24. M. E. MNYAMPALA, *Mashairi ya hekima na malumbano ya ushairi*, Dar es Salaam, p. 15.

25. For further details see the *Linguistic Reporter*, 8/3, June 1966.

26. Thus providing confirmation for M. B. Nsimbi's view in 'The

Future of Vernacular Literature in Uganda', *EACH*, pp. 95–102, where there is no reference to Swahili at all.

27. Jumuiya ya kustawisha Kiswahili, *Kiongozi*, 1 October 1964.

28. 'Wanachama wanaamini kabisa kwamba kufahamu asili ya kitu ndio hasa kuelewa ubora wa kitu hicho na ndio msingi wa kukipenda na kukiheshimu', *Kiongozi*, 1 October 1964.

29. As, for example, in 'Tengeneza Kiswahili', *Ngurumo*, 8 January 1966.

CHAPTER VII

1. E. HAUGEN, 'Planning for a Standard Language in Modern Norway', *Anthrop. Ling*, Vol. I, 1959, p. 8.

1a. PAUL KRATOCHVIL, *The Chinese Language To-day*, Hutchinson, 1968, pp. 135–6.

2. U. HEYD, *Language Reform in Modern Turkey*, Oriental Notes and Studies, No. 5, Jerusalem, 1954, p. 51.

3. In this respect the financial help given by the Ministry of Education to the 1966 Workshop on Primary Courses in Swahili was a most encouraging augury.

4. For a somewhat different appraisal see L. Harries's 'Swahili in Modern East Africa'. (See reference on p. 113)

5. I am grateful to the Editor of the *Journal of African Languages* for permission to reproduce material from my 'Problems of a lingua franca: Swahili and the Trade Unions', *J.A.L.*, 3, 1964 in the following two paragraphs.

6. I am grateful to Mr J. L. Brain of the University of Syracuse for the following note: '. . . In Tanganyika I first heard the word *chama* applied to women's clubs, not to political organizations, whereas these are called *kilabu* in Kenya. *Kilabu* in most of Tanganyika only means a beer club. . . .' The origin of the word *chama* is obscure, but it is probably cognate with *njama* a 'secret meeting', and with similar words in other Bantu languages of this area.

7. 'Wakati huu nchini Afrika hakuna siasa ya kupingana, lakini siasa ambayo ili(y)oko ni ya kupinga Wabeberu pamoja na kujenga Taifa la Kiafrika . . .', *Mfanyi Kazi*, 23 January 1963.

8. 'Ni lazima kila jambo kufanywa katika Afrika hakukuwa na upinzani . . .', *Mfanyi Kazi*, 23 January 1963.

9. (1) Watu wengi katika nchi waliweza kupata uchumi wao katika kupanda tumbako, kahawa, mazomba na mihindi.

(2) Ninaposikia neno hili uchumi, ninaelewa kuwa ni mali au

raslimali ipatikanayo katika nchi ili kuiwezesha nchi hiyo iwe na maendeleo

(3) Kwa nchi yetu hii ya Tanzania uchumi wake unapatikana hasa juu ya kilimo pamoja na madini

(4) Fungu la kwanza ambalo tunaweza kuingiza uchumi katika nchi yetu ni ukulima

(5) Zaidi ya hayo mabasi ya abiria huleta uchumi lakini kama njia zingelikuwa mbaya. . . .

(6) Uchumi ni kazi ya kila siku ya mtu binafsi au jumuiya ya watu wakishirikiana pamoja kwa kufanya kazi ye yote yenye kuleta pato

(7) Wanafunzi walio na ujuzi wa uchumi waliofukuzwa mwaka huu, walileta hasara kubwa nchini badala ya uchumi

(8) Uchumi ni rasimali [sic] ya shamba lako au kitu chochote kinacho kuletea uchumi juu ya rasimali yako. . . .

(9) Maana ya uchumi ni mazao yanayolimwa katikanchi yako. . . .

(10) Makabila mengi yanajuwa jinsi uchumi unavyopatikan, pia wanajua jinsi unavyofanywa na wengi pia hufanya uchumi mwingi wa namna mbalimbali kukuza nchi zao

10. *Uchumi wetu 1965 hadi 1967*, Mpiga chapa wa Serikali, 1966. *Our Economy 1965–1967*, Govt. Printer, 1966

11. *The Arusha Declaration and TANU's Policy on Socialism and Self-reliance*, TANU Publicity Section, 1967, p. 1. *Azimio la Arusha na Siasa ya TANU juu ya Ujamaa na kujitegemea*, Idara ya Habari, TANU, 1967.

12. Though the appearance of books like Peter Temu's *Uchumi Bora*, O.U.P., 1966, will do something to help.

13. 'The Future of Swahili Literature', *East Africa's Cultural Heritage*, Contemporary African Monograph Series, 4, EAPH, 1966, p. 93.

14. See O. Wali's 'The Daed End of African Literature', *Transition*, 10, 1963, 13–15, and the vigorous discussion which this provoked in succeeding issues of this journal.

If original writing is lacking there has been a marked increase in the number of translations: George Orewell's *Animal Farm* has proved popular, and translations of the novels of Chinua Achebe and the Kenyan, James Ngugi, are also in preparation.

Select Bibliography on Swahili Language

The most detailed bibliography to date is the recently published *Practical and Systematical Swahili Bibliography, Linguistics 1850–1963*, compiled by Marcel Van Spaandonck, Leiden, 1965, and the supplement by Alberto Mioni in *Cahiers d'Etudes Africaines*, Vol. 27, 1967, 485–532.

ASHTON, E. O. 'The "Idea" Approach to Swahili', *B.S.O.(A.)S.* Vol. VII, 1936, 837–59.

ASHTON, E. O. 'The Structure of a Bantu Language with Special Reference to Swahili, or Form and Function through Bantu Eyes', *B.S.O.(A.)S.* Vol. VIII, 1937, 111–20.

ASHTON, E. O. *Swahili Grammar* (including intonation), London, 1944.

BERNANDER, E. *De första grunderma i Swahili*, Scandinavian Institute of African Studies, Uppsala, 1964.

BINNS, H. K. *Swahili–English Dictionary*, S.P.C.K., 1925. (A revision of Krapf's dictionary.)

BRAIN, J. L. *Basic Structure of Swahili*, Syracuse University, 1965 (cyclostyled).

BRAUNER, S., and BANTU, J. K. *Lehrbuch des Swahili*, VEB Verlag Enzyklopädie, Leipzig, 1964.

BROOMFIELD, G. W. *Sarufi ya Kiswahili*, London, 1931.

BRUTEL, E. *Grammaire élémentaire du Kiswahili*, Bruxelles, 1921.

BRYAN, M. A. *Swahili Pocket Dictionary*, London, 1948.

BURT, F. *Swahili Grammar and Vocabulary* (Kimvita Dialect), S.P.C.K., 1910.

BÜTTNER, C. G. *Wörterbuch der Suaheli–Sprache, Suaheli–Deutsch und Deutsch–Suaheli*, Stuttgart, 1890.

CARCOFORO, E. *Elementi di Somali e Ki-Suaheli parlati al Benadir*, Milan, 1912.

DAULL, P. A. *Grammaire de Kisouahili*, Paris, 1879.

DELAUNAY, P. *Dictionnaire Français–Kiswahili*, Paris, 1885.

DELIUS, S. *Grammatik der Suaheli–Sprache*, Tanga, 1910, and Berlin, 1928.

EBERLE, E. *Kiswahili*, Olten, 1953.

ELPHINSTONE, SIR HOWARD. *Road to Swahili*, Nairobi, 1946.

EYNDE, F. VAN DEN. *Grammaire Swahili*, Bruxelles, 1944.

FIEDOROVA, N. G. *A Swahili Text-book*, Moscow, 1963.

FIEDOROVA, N. G. 'Some Ways of Noun-building in Swahili', *African Philology*, Moscow, 1965.

GROMOVA, N. V. 'The Swahili Language', *Asia and Africa Today*, 1963.

GROMOVA, N. V. 'On the Principles of Defining the Noun as a Part of Speech in Swahili', *African Philology*, Moscow, 1965.

HADDON, E. B. *Swahili Lessons*, Cambridge, 1955.

HARRIS, Z. 'The Phonemes of Swahili' (being an appendix to Chapters 7–9 in *Methods in Structural Linguistics*, Chicago, 1951).

HEEPE, M. 'Alte Verbalformen mit vollständiger Vokalassimilation im Suaheli', *Z.F.K.*, Vol. IX, 1918–19.

HEEPE, M. *Die Komoren-Dialekte Ngazidja, Nzwani und Mwali*, Hamburg, 1920.

HÖFTMANN, H. *Suaheli–Deutsches Wörterbuch*, Leipzig, 1963.

JOHNSON, F. *A Standard English–Swahili and a Standard Swahili–English Dictionary* (2 vols.), O.U.P., 1939.

Journal of the East African Swahili Committee (J.E.A.S.C.). Nos. 1–5 cyclostyled. Nos. 6–23 printed under the title of *Bulletin of the Inter-Territorial Language (Swahili) Committee*. Nos. 24–29/1 under the above title. 29/1 onwards under the title of *Swahili*, Journal of the East African Swahili Committee until the East African Swahili Committee was absorbed by the Institute of Swahili Research in 1965.

KOPOKA, O. B. *Vihusiano. Sarufi na Ufasaha I*, Kampala, 1955.

KOPOKA, O. B. *Miao. Sarufi na Ufasaha II*, Kampala, 1956.

KOUTUZOV, A. I. *A Russian–Swahili Newspaper Vocabulary*, Moscow, 1963.

KOUTUZOV, A. I. *Swahili–Russian and Russian–Swahili Dictionary*, Moscow, 1965.

KOUZNETSOV, P. S. *A Vocabulary of Political Terminology*, Moscow, 1933–4.

KOUZNETSOV, P. S. 'On Noun Classification and the System of Grammatical Agreement in Swahili', The Scientific Research Association for Studying National and Colonial Problems, Vol. XIX, *Foreign Oriental Languages, N.I.*, Moscow, 1935.

KOUZNETSOV, P. S. 'On the Number of Noun Classes in Swahili', *African Philology*, Moscow, 1955.

KRAPF, J. L. *Outline of the Elements of the Ki-Suaheli Language with Special Reference to the Kinika Dialect*, Tübingen, 1850.

KRAPF, J. L. *A Dictionary of the Swahili Language*, London, 1882.

KRUMM, B. *Words of Oriental Origin in Swahili*, London, 1940.

LAMBERT, H. E. *Ki-Vumba, A Dialect of the Southern Kenya Coast*, Kampala, 1957.

LAMBERT, H. E. *Chi-Jomvu and Ki-Ngare, Sub-dialects of the Mombasa Area*, Kampala, 1958.

LAMBERT, H. E. *Chi-Chifundi, A Dialect of the Southern Kenya Coast*, Kampala, 1958.

LOOGMAN, A. *Swahili Grammar and Syntax*, Pittsburg, Pa., Duquesne University Press (Duquesne Studies Afr. Series 1), 1965.

MADAN, A. C. *English–Swahili Dictionary*, London, 1894.

MADAN, A. C. *Swahili–English Dictionary*, 1903.

MADAN, A. C. *Swahili (Zanzibar) Grammar*, 1905.

MEINHOF, C. 'Die Sprache der Suaheli in Deutsch-Ostafrika', *A.D.K.S.* Vol. II, 1910.

MIACHINA, E. N. 'On Verb-indications in Swahili', *Works on African Ethnography*, Vol. III, 1959.

MIACHINA, E. N. 'Formatives in Swahili', *African Ethnographic Collection*, 1959.

MIACHINA, E. N. *Swahili*, Moscow, 1960.

MIACHINA, E. N. 'The Accentuated Suffixes in Swahili', *African Ethnographic Collection*, Vol. 90, 6, 1966.

MISIUGIN, V. M. 'Origin of Dissemination of the Swahili Language'. (One of a collection of essays relating to Africa in the *Proceedings of the Ethnographic Institute of the U.S.S.R.*, Vol. L, 11, 1959, Moscow.)

NATALIS, E. *La langue Swahili 1. cours méthodique 2. Exercices*, F.U.L.R.E.A.C., Liège, 1960.

OHLY, R. 'Abstract Nouns within the System of Noun Class 14 in Swahili', *Rocznik Orientalstyczny* Vol. XXIX, 2, Warsaw, 1965.

OHLY, R. 'Exocentric function of noun in Swahili' *Africana Bulletin*, 5, Warsaw, 1966, 93–104.

OKHOTINA, N. V., FIEDOROVA, N. G., and YAKOVLEVA, I. P. *A Russian–Swahili Conversation-book*, Moscow, 1963.

OKHOTINA, N. V. 'The Morphemic Structure of the Verb in Swahili', *ference on Typology of Oriental Languages*, Moscow, 1963.

OKHOTINA, N. V. 'Principles Underlying Analysis of the Morphemic Structure of the Word in Swahili', *The Peoples of Asia and Africa*, 6. 1964.

OKHOTINA, N. V. 'The Morphemic Structure of Noun and Verb in Swahili', *African Philology*, Moscow, 1965.

OLDEROGGE, D. A. *Swahili–Russian and Russian–Swahili Dictionary*,

Soviet Academy of Sciences, 1961. (With a grammatical appendix by E. N. Miachina.)

PERROTT, D. V. *Teach Yourself Swahili*, London, 1951.

PETRYANKINA, V. I. 'A Comparative Investigation of Vocalism in Russian and Swahili', *Transactions of the Moscow Regional Pedagogical Institute*, Vol. CXXXIX, 9, 1963.

PETRYANKINA, V.I. 'The Classification of Russian and Swahili Consonant Phonemes', *Transactions of the Moscow Regional Pedagogical Institute*, Vol. CXXXIX, 9, 1963.

PICK, V. M. *Grammatica della lingua Swahili*, Torino, 1953.

PICK, V. M. *Vocabolario Swahili–Italiano e Italiano–Swahili*, Torino, 1964.

POLOMÉ, E. 'Geographical Differences in Lexical Usage in Swahili', 2nd. Int. Cong. of Dialectologists, Marburg, 1965.

POLOMÉ, E. *Swahili Language Handbook*, CAL, 1967.

RŮŽIČKA, K. F. 'Lehnwörter im Swahili', *A.O.*, Vol. XXI, 1953.

RŮŽIČKA, K. F. 'Infinitive in Swahili', *A.O.*, Vol. XXIV, 1–2, 1956.

SACHEDINA, A. J. *Gujarati–Swahili Shabdakosh*, Dar es Salaam, 1954.

SACLEUX, C. *Grammaire des Dialectes Swahilis*, Paris, 1909.

SACLEUX, C. *Grammaire Swahilie*, 1909.

SACLEUX, C. *Dictionnaire Swahili–Français, Français–Swahili*, Vol. I, 1939, Vol. II, 1941, Paris.

SEIDEL, A. *Eine praktische Grammatik der Suaheli-Sprache*, Wien, 1890.

SEIDEL, A. *Suaheli Konversations-Grammatik*, Heidelberg, 1900; 2nd edn., Heidelberg, 1941.

SNOXALL, R. A. *A Concise English–Swahili Dictionary* (Kamusi ya Kiingereza–Kiswahili), London, 1958.

STEERE, E. *A Handbook of the Swahili Language as Spoken at Zanzibar*, London, 1870.

STEERE, E. *Swahili Exercises*, U.M.C.A., Zanzibar, 1878; London, 1886.

STEERE, E. *Swahili Handbook*, Revised by Canon A. B. Hellier, London, 1950.

STEERE, E. *Swahili Exercises*, Revised by Canon A. B. Hellier, 1934 and 1951.

STEVICK, E. W. AND OTHERS. *Swahili Basic Course*, Foreign Service Inst., Washington, D.C., 1963.

STROGANOVA, I. P. 'The Process of Noun Classification Development in the Bantu Languages', *Transactions of Leningrad University*, 1952.

TAYLOR, W. E. *The Groundwork of the Swahili Language*, 1898.

TRIVEDI, B. V. *Gujarati–Swahili Dictionary* (Gujarati–Swahili Shabdapothi), 1955.

TUCKER, A. N., and ASHTON, E. O. 'Swahili Phonetics', *African Studies*, Vol. I, 1942, 77–182.

TUCKER, A. N. 'Foreign Sounds in Swahili', *B.S.O.(A.)S.*, Vol. XI, 4, and Vol. XII, 1, 1946–7.

VELTEN, C. *Praktische Suaheli-Grammatik*, 1904.

VELTEN, C. *Suaheli-Sprachführer für Postbeamte*, 1910.

VELTEN, C. *Suaheli–Wörterbuch, Part I, Suaheli–Deutsch*, 1910.

WEGHSTEEN, J. *Ki-Swahili (Sarufi na kazi za sarufi)*, Albertville. 4th edn., 1953.

WERNER, A. *A First Swahili Book*, London, 1927.

WHITEHEAD, J. and L. F. *Manuel de Kingwana*, Lualaba, Congo Belge, 1928.

WHITELEY, W. H. 'Kimvita. An Inquiry into Dialectal Status and Characteristics', *J.E.A.S.C.*, Vol. 25, 1955, 10–38.

WHITELEY, W. H. *Ki-Mtang'ata – A Dialect of the Mrima Coast, Tanganyika*, Kampala, 1956.

WHITELEY, W. H. *An Introduction to the Dialects and Verse of Pemba*, Kampala, 1958.

WHITELEY, W. H. 'An Introduction to the Rural Dialects of Zanzibar, Part I' *Swahili*, Vol. 30, 1959, 41–70.

WHITELEY, W. H. 'An Introduction to the Rural Dialects of Zanzibar, Part II, Texts, Riddles and Word–list', *Swahili*, Vol. 31, 1960, 200–18.

WHITELEY, W. H. 'Some Problems of the Syntax of Sentences in a Bantu Language of East Africa', *Lingua*, Vol. IX, 2, 1960, 148–74.

WHITELEY, W. H. 'Further Problems in the Study of Swahili Sentences', *Lingua*, Vol. X, 2, 1961, 148–73.

WHITELEY, W. H. 'Notes on the Chi-Miini Dialect of Swahili', *ALS*, Vol. VI, 1965, 67–72.

WHITELEY, W. H. *Some problems of Transitivity in Swahili*, School of Oriental and African Studies, London, 1968.

YAKOVLEVA, I. P. 'Sketches on the Syntax of Swahili', *Works on African Ethnography*, Vol. III, 1959.

NOTE: Russian titles have been translated into English, but the two Polish ones are both originally in English.

Index

Publications are italicized or in quotation marks as in the text.

* Indicates language entries.   † Indicates entries of peoples.

ABDULAZIZ, M. H., 38
Abedi, Sheikh Amri, 105
Africa, viii
Akilimali Snowwhite, K. H. A., 126
Ali ibn al-Husain, 34
Ali, Sheikh Mohamed, 107
al-Idrisi, 28–9, 31
Allen, J. W. T., 16, 17, 93, 109
al-Mas'udi, 32, 34
Angoya, 36
Ankole, 70
Arabic,* 7, 28–9, 55, 75, 77, 106
  and early history of Swahili, 2, 31,
    34, 36, 38
  and Swahili verse, 13, 17, 18, 42
  status of, 8, 39
Ashton, Mrs E. O., 16
Association for the Advancement of
  Swahili, 110, 112

Bagamoyo, 4, 52, 53, 58
Baganda,† 11, 69, 70
Bajun,† 4
Bangwana,† 72
Bantu languages,* 3, 4, 7, 16, 71
  early history of, 29–40 *passim*
  in Belgian Congo, 73, 75
  Swahili as, 8, 9, 111
Baramaji,* 52
Barazani, 60
Barbosa, Duarte, 36
Belgian Congo, 1, 57, 89
  educational policies in,   72–6
    passim
  see also Congo
Bemba,* 30, 31
Bismarck, Otto von, 57
Blanket Boy's Moon, 67
Bondei,† 57
Boondei,* 55
Brava, 2, 4, 77
Broomfield, G. W., 16, 85, 87
Buganda, 11, 46, 69, 70, 71
Bujumbura, 3, 52
Bunyoro, 70
Burton, Sir R. F., 45, 47, 49, 50, 52

Burundi, 3, 14
Busaidi,† 25, 42
Bushiri,† 24, 57, 91
Busoga, 70
Büttner, C. G., 13, 17, 59
Bweni, 58

Cape Delgado, 3
Cary, Joyce, 10
Chaga,† 12
Chaga,* 100, 114
Chairman Mao, 15
'Changing Position of Swahili in
    East Africa', viii
Chi-Chifundi,* 4, 24, 91
Chi-Jomvu,* 4, 6, 24, 91
Chi-Miini,* 4, 77
Church Missionary Society (C.M.S.),
    11, 49, 53, 54, 69, 80, 81
Chwa, Sir Daudi, 70
Comoro Islands, 37, 39, 45, 89
  dialects of, 4
  educational policies in,   76–7
    passim
Congo, 3, 52, 91, 99
  dialects of, 5
  see also Belgian Congo
Consolata Missions, 14
Costermansville, 74

Dammann, E., 13, 17
Dar es Salaam, 9, 14, 31, 52, 58, 60,
    62, 64, 67, 106, 111
  and East African Swahili Com-
    mittee, 79, 82, 84, 90, 93
  University College of, 38, 97, 102,
    105, 108, 109, 110
de Courteille, P., 32
de Meynard, C. B., 32
Dengereko,† 52
'Development of Ki-Swahili as an
    Educational and Administra-
    tive Language in the Uganda
    Protectorate', 70
dos Santos, Father, 36

East African Institute of Social Research, 90
East African Literature Bureau, 88, 89, 90
East African Swahili Committee, 16, 60, 71, 79, 82–93 *passim*, 109
  and *Bulletin*, 85, 90, 91, 92, 93
  and *Journal*, 91, 92, 109
  and *Swahili*, 92
el-Buhry family, 17, 24
Eliot, Sir Charles, 65
Elizabethville, 2, 74
Exercises (Hellier), 15
Exercises (Steere), 15

Faza, 39
  and Swahili literature, 2, 7, 42
Fuller, Susan, 8
Freeman-Grenville, Dr G. S. P., viii, 32–4, 38
Frere Town, 80

Galla,† 1
Ganda,* 31, 69, 71
German East Africa, 13, 57
  see also Tanganyika
Gindo,† 52
Gisu,* 116
Goa, 38
Gogo,* 9, 114
Gowers, Sir W. F., 70
Guillain, M., 44, 50, 51, 52
Guthrie, Professor M., 29–30

Ha,* 9
Ha,† 61
Habari za Mwezi, 60
Habari za Wakilindi, 60
Hadimu,† 6
Handbook (Hellier), 15
Handbook of the Swahili Language, 15, 53
Hamziya, 18
Harries, Dr L., 17, 18, 74, 75, 76
Hasan bin Omari, 58
Hausa,* 10
Haya,† 12
Haya,* 100, 114
Hehe,† 58
Hellier, A. B., 15
Hemedi b. Abdulla b. Said el-Buhry, 24
History of Kilwa, 34–8 *passim*
Holy Ghost Mission, 13, 53
'How the Different Races in Zanzibar speak Swahili', 5

Ibn Battuta, 35, 36
Institute of Swahili Research, 82, 84, 93, 108, 109, 111

Inter-Territorial Language (Swahili) Committee, *see* East African Swahili Committee
Irgobawe, 63
Islam, 2, 25, 39, 69, 73, 81
  and Swahili literature, 18, 24, 101
  language of, 8, 39
Itawa, 47

Johnson, Frederick, 16, 84
Journal of the American Oriental Society, 50
Julius Caesar, 126

KADU, 68
Kamba,* 31, 68
Kampala, 97
KANU, 68
Karagwe, 52
Katanga, 72, 73, 75
Kawawa, Rashidi M., 120
Kenya, vii, 2, 14, 21, 31, 55, 71, 77, 89, 98, 109, 116, 119, 125
  and Swahili literature, 18, 24, 65
  dialects of, 3, 4, 6
  educational policies in, 57, 65–8, 80, 81, 82, 85
  language choice in, viii, 99
  opposition to Swahili in, 12
Ki-Amu,* 4
Kidasi, K. Z., 106
Ki-Hadimu,* 4, 91
Ki-Hindi,* 5
Kiimbila, J. K., 106
Kikuyu,† 12
Kikuyu,* 14, 31, 67, 68
Kilwa, 25, 38, 39, 45, 52, 58
  see also *History of Kilwa*
Ki-Mtang'ata,* 4, 6, 91
Ki-Mvita,* 4, 7, 38
Ki-Ngare,* 4, 6, 24, 91
Kingwana,* 5, 72, 74, 75, 76
Kinkwhere,* 52
Kinshasa, 3
Ki-Nzwani,* 4, 76
Kiongozi, 106
Ki-Pate,* 4
Ki-Pemba,* 7
Ki-Settla,* 5, 65
Ki-Shela,* 4
Ki-Siu,* 4
Kitab Rujar, 28
Ki-Tikuu,* 4
Ki-Tumbatu,* 4, 91
Kiungani, 57
Kiunguja,* 77, 86
Ki-Vumba,* 4, 91
Knappert, Dr J., 29, 33–4, 93, 109
  and Swahili literature, 17, 18, 19
Kondoa, 58

Kongo,* 30, 72, 73
Kopoka, O. B., 91
Krapf, J. L., 2, 16, 17, 49, 55, 80
   his grammar and dictionary, 13, 53
Kratochvil, Paul, 117
Kulichi, 62
Kulubya, S., 71

La Langue swahilie, 76
Lake Nyasa, 52, 53, 80
Lake Tanganyika, 46, 73, 80
Lake Victoria, 9, 52, 53
Lambert, H. E., viii, 16, 17, 88, 90, 91
Lamo,* 52
Lamu, 4, 42, 43
   and Swahili literature, 7, 25
'Language and Politics in East Africa', viii
Leopold II, 72
Leopoldville, 72
Lief ben Saied, 49
Lingala,*, 72, 73
London Missionary Society, 53
Luba,* 30, 72, 73, 75
Luganda,* 11, 69, 71
Luo,† 12, 71
Luo,* 68

Madagascar, 45, 54, 77
Madan, A. C., 15, 16, 84
Mafia, 39
   dialect of, 4
Magila, 53, 60
Makonde,† 52
Makua,† 36, 57
Malawi, 31, 77
Malindi, 36, 39
Mambo Leo, 63, 80
Maniema, 74
Mara Gazeti, 63
Masai,† vii, 53
Masasi, 53
Masury, S. K., 49
Matumbi,† 52
Mauritius, 45
Mazrui,† 21, 25, 42, 46, 58
Mboamaji, 52
Mbulu, 61
'Medieval Evidence for Swahili', 32
Meinhof, Professor C., 13, 80
Memoirs of the American Academy, 49
Mfanyi Kazi, 120
Mikindani, 42
Mkwawa, 58

Mnyampala, M. E., 111, 126
Mogadishu, 25, 35
Muhammed Said Abdullah, 126
Mombasa, 1, 35, 39, 46, 49, 52, 82, 93
   and Swahili literature, 7, 19, 21, 23, 24, 42–3, 81
   dialects of, 4, 6, 8, 15, 52, 53, 80–1, 91, 115–16 *passim*
Mongo,* 73
Monjou,* 1
Morice, M., 37, 44, 45
Morogoro, 13
Mozambique, 2, 3, 36, 44
Mpwapwa, 53, 54
Mrima coast, 58
Msimulizi, 60
Mtang'ata, 4
Mudoe,† 52
Mugdasho, 1
Muhammed bin Abdullah, 21
Mulcaster, Roger, 94
Munisi, S. E., 28
Mushi, S., 104
Musophilus, 94
Mutesa, 69
Muyaka bin Haji al-Ghassaniy, 2, 19–20, 42, 58
Mwangaza, 63
Mwanza, 52
Mzigra,† 52

Nabhani,† 25
Nairobi, 52, 64, 65, 66, 67, 82, 90, 97, 99, 125
Natalis, E., 14, 76
National Swahili Council, *see* Tanzania
Nationalist, The, 28, 32, 97
Nchi Yetu, 107
Neno la Amani, 76
Ngazija,* 4, 76, 77
Ngoni,† 53
Ngurumo, 110, 120, 121
Nilotes,† 65, 71
Nilotic languages, 3, 7
Northern Rhodesia, 89
Nyakyusa,* 61, 100, 114
Nyamwezi,* 9, 54
Nyamwezi,† 52, 60
Nyankore,* 31
Nyankunde, 76
Nyasaland, 89
Nyassa,† 57
Nyerere, President, 65, 119, 126
Nyoro,* 31

Odinga, O., 119
Olderogge, Professor D. A., 14

Oliver, Professor Roland, 30
Oman, 20, 46
Orwell, George,
  and *1984*, 93
*Outline of the Elements of the Kisua-
  heli Language with Special
  Reference to the Kinika Dialect*,
  49

Pangani, 58
Panjim, 38
Passionist Fathers, 14
Pate, 4, 39, 42, 43
  and Swahili literature, 18, 25
Payton, William, 37, 51
Periplus, 30
Perrott, D. V., 16
Pemba, 4, 35, 39
  and Swahili literature, 7, 22–5
  dialects of, 6, 91
Polomé, E. C., 17, 74
Prince Kombo, 38
'Problems of a lingua franca:
  Swahili and the Trade Unions',
  viii
Ptolemy, 30
Pwani na Bara, 60

Rafiki Yangu, 60
Ratcliffe, B. J., 16, 84, 88
Rechenberg, Freiherr von, 59
Ribe, 80
Robert, Shaaban, ix, 10, 94, 125
Roberts, Edmund, 44, 46
Rosberg, Carl, 68
Ross Browne, J., 50, 51, 52
Rwanda, 3, 14

Saadani, 52, 58
Sacleux, Fr Charles, 13, 16, 17, 29
Sagara,† 52
Salt, Henry, 1, 2, 7, 50, 51
Schnee, H., 59
Segeju,† 36
Seidel, A., 13, 59
Seychelles, 45
Seyyid Barghash, 20
Seyyid Said, 20, 45, 46
Sheikh Mbaruk bin Rashid, 21
Shambala,† 54, 60
Sindh, 52
Smee, Capt. T., 50, 51
Snoxall, R. A., 16, 17, 88
Society for the Enhancement of the
  Swahili Language and Verse,
  111
Socotra, 77
Somalia, 3, 4, 77, 89

Somauli,† 1
Sowauli,† 1
*Standard Swahili–English, English–
  Swahili Dictionary*, 16
Stanley, H. M., 69
Stanleyville, 2, 73, 74
Steere, Bishop Edward, 15, 53, 54,
  55, 79
Sukuma,* 31
Sukuma,† 61
Suleiman bin Nasor Lemky, 23
Suud bin Said al-Maamiry, 21
Swahili–English Dictionary, 84
Swahili Grammar, 16
*Swahili–Russian, Russian–Swahili
  Dictionary*, 14
Swedish Missions, 14

Tabora, 3, 46, 52, 53
Talut ibn al-Husain, 34
Tanga, 53, 55, 58, 110
  and Swahili literature, 24
  education in, 59
Tanganyika, 11, 52, 55, 67, 68, 86,
  89, 91, 121
  educational policies in, 57–65
    passim, 79, 80, 81, 82
  opposition to Swahili in, 12
  see also German East Africa
Tanganyika Notes, viii
TANU, 62, 65, 124
Tanzania, 3, 9, 15, 31, 52
  and missions, 14
  and national language policy, 1,
    93, 99–112, 114–15, 117–26
    passim
  and National Swahili Council, 112
  and Swahili literature, 65
  dialects of, 4
Taylor, W. E., 15, 17
Tazama, 67
Teach Yourself Swahili, 16
Time Educational Supplement, 8
Tippu Tip, vii, 46, 47, 72, 74, 91
Tongoni, 6, 24, 91
Toro, 70
Travels of Marco Polo, 28

Uganda, vii, 3, 31, 52, 53, 55, 80, 89,
  98, 109
  Anglicans in, 11
  educational policies in, 57, 69–72,
    82, 99, 116
  Rwenzururu movement in, 116
Uganda News, 70
Ugogo, 52
Uhehe, 52
Uhuru, 106, 112
Ujiji, 3, 46, 52, 53

United Republic of Tanzania, *see* Tanzania
Universities' Mission to Central Africa (U.M.C.A.), 11, 42, 53, 55, 57, 60, 80
Unyamwezi, 46
Urungu, 47
Utenzi wa Mikidadi na Mayasa, 19
Utenzi wa Tambuka, 38–9

Vanga, 4
Velten, Carl, 13, 47, 58, 59
Vignard, G., 50, 51, 52
von Ewald, H., 49
von Gabelentz, H. C., 49
Voyage to Abyssinia and Travels, 1
Vumba, 6, 24
Vyama vya Wafanya Kazi, 120

Wainwright, G. A., 33
Werner, Alice, 6
Werner, Misses, A. & M., 15, 17, 79
Weston, Professor A. B., 105
White Fathers, 53, 69
Whitehead, 14

Wilson, J. L., 49
Winde, 58
Wolsey, Cardinal, 21
Woodward, H. W., 55
Wright, Marcia, 11

Yakovleva, I. P., 15
Yao,† 57
Yao,* 31, 54

Zambia, 3, 30, 31, 52
Zanzibar, vii, 5, 13, 20, 39, 42, 55, 57, 58, 72, 80, 82, 89, 104, 109, 126
and Swahili literature, 24, 25
as trading centre, 44–7, 49, 54
dialects of, 4, 6, 8, 52, 53, 80, 91
Marco Polo, 28
Zeitschrift der Deutschen Morgenländischen Gesellschaft, 49
Zendjs,† 35
Zimba,† 36
Zuhra, 62
Zulu,* 98